Publisher's Note

Were UFOs not a world-wide phenomenon in scope, extent and observation, V&S Publishers would not have considered publishing this book. According to reliable reports this phenomenon has been witnessed in 133 different countries. Indeed, it has touched on the lives of an increasing number of people around the world.

The sightings are so strange and foreign to our daily mode of thinking that it is frequently countered by ridicule and derision by persons and organizations not acquainted with the facts. Yet, the phenomenon persists; it has not faded away as many of us expected it would when, years ago, we regarded it as a passing fad.

UFOs... Unidentified Flying Objects... which is defined as any aerial or surface sighting, or instrumental recording (e.g., photography, radar, etc.) remains unexplained even after examination by qualified persons. Nonetheless, in the popular mind the UFO phenomenon is associated with the concept of extra-terrestrial intelligence and this might yet prove to be correct in some context. Surely it would be a big joke on all of us should it develop that proof for extra-terrestrial intelligence was here right under our noses all the time while we were searching for it elsewhere!

The terms Flying Saucers and UFOs now appear in the dictionaries of many countries... itself a sure sign of the popular awareness. UFO reports in significant numbers have been made by persons in responsible positions: astronauts, commercial pilots, radar experts, and military men... officials of governments, and astronomers, and even scientists!

Perhaps the most difficult-to-believe data comes from the so-called Close Encounters of one Kind or the other. These are the cases in which there appears physical evidence of the presence of the UFO in immediate surroundings. This can take the form of immediate physical effects on either animate or inanimate matter, or on both. Thus, physiological effects on humans and animals and plants have been very reliably reported, as have the interference with electrical and machinery systems in the immediate vicinity. More than one thousand physical trace cases are on record.

In our considered opinion, the UFO phenomenon is real and not the creation of disturbed minds, and that it may have important communications for science and for the social well-being of the peoples of this Earth.

Who can tell what benefits might accrue from the study of UFOs? It might well lead to the solution of many pressing problems facing humankind today.

In case you have observed any, do write to us about the event in detail!

We hope you enjoy the thrill of reading the findings as reported in newspapers and journals!

UFO CASE FILES

Scintillating Encounters with ET & Mysterious Aliens

V&S PUBLISHERS

Published by:

F-2/16, Ansari Road, Daryaganj, New Delhi-110002
011-23240026, 011-23240027 • *Fax:* 011-23240028
Email: info@vspublishers.com • *Website:* www.vspublishers.com

Branch : Hyderabad
5-1-707/1, Brij Bhawan (Beside Central Bank of India Lane)
Bank Street, Koti, Hyderabad - 500 095
040-24737290
E-mail: vspublishershyd@gmail.com

Follow us on:

For any assistance sms **VSPUB** to **56161**
All books available at **www.vspublishers.com**

© **Copyright:** V&S PUBLISHERS
ISBN 978-93-505702-2-7
Edition 2013

The Copyright of this book, as well as all matter contained herein (including illustrations) rests with the Publishers. No person shall copy the name of the book, its title design, matter and illustrations in any form and in any language, totally or partially or in any distorted form. Anybody doing so shall face legal action and will be responsible for damages.

Printed at : Param Offseters, Okhla, New Delhi-110020

Contents

Publisher's Note 3
Introduction 7
UFO Encounters Classification 9

1. Lt. Gorman's Dogfight 11
2. Kenneth Arnold Sighting 15
3. The Death of Thomas Mantell 17
4. The Chiles/Whitted Sighting 22
5. The Lubbock Lights 25
6. The Fort Monmouth UFO Case 28
7. Operation Mainbrace Sightings 31
8. B-29 Crew Encounters UFOs 34
9. The Sea Fury Incident 36
10. US Senators see Flying Saucers in Soviet Russia 39
11. UFO Interest in Nuclear Tests 42
12. The Levelland, Texas Landings 44
13. Frightened Dog Case 48
14. An Astronaut Speaks Out 50
15. The Warminster Thing 54
16. Florida Everglades Encounter 56
17. The Tully Saucer Nest 59
18. Bizarre UFO Encounter over Texas Uranium Mine 63
19. Soviet Cosmonaut sees Close-Up of UFO 65
20. Hudson Valley Sightings 67
21. Japanese Airline 1628 Encounters UFO 70
22. Florida Police Patrolman Encounters UFO 75
23. St. Petersburg, Russia Incident 77

Alien Encounters 79

1. Voronezh, Russia UFO Landing and Aliens 80
2. The Alfred Burtoo Encounter 83
3. Forester Encounters Mine-like Entities in Scotland
   (the Dechmont Woods Encounter) 86

4. UFO with Two Occupants Hovers over Man's Car 90
5. Occupant Encounter in Argentina 92
6. UFO with Humanoid Encountered by Two Forestry Workers in Finland 96
7. UFO and Occupants seen near Cowichan Hospital in BC, Canada 99
8. Milakovic Family Encounter, Hanbury, England 102
9. Valensole, France Landing (Maurice Masse Case) 104
10. Socorro/Zamora UFO Incident.. 106
11. Eagle River Close Encounter (Man given 'Pancakes' by UFO Occupants) 110
12. Father Gill / Papua New Guinea Sighting........................ 115
13. The Kelly-Hopkinsville 'Goblins' Encounter 123
14. The Flatwoods Monster... 126
15. Man Encounters Humanoids at Varese, Italy (The Bruno Facchini Case) 129
16. The Villa Santina Case (Two Humanoids Encountered by Italian Artist)... 132

Alien Abductions 134

1. Villas Boas Case 137
2. Betty and Barney Hill Case 143
3. The Betty Andreasson Encounter 149
4. Police Patrolman Herbert Schirmer Abduction................ 152
5. Abduction of José Antonio da Silva 155
6. Abduction at Medicine Bow National Park 157
7. Man Taken into Craft, Encounter with Three Beings 160
8. Travis Walton Abduction Case 165
9. Police Constable Alan Godfrey's Abduction in West Yorkshire, England.. 169
10. The Salter Encounter... 173
11. Kelly Cahill Abduction 176
12. World-Wide Abduction Cases... 180

Introduction

Unidentified flying object (UFO) is a strange light or object that appears in the sky or near the ground. Its existence defies scientific explanation. Some people believe UFO's may be spaceships from other planets. Others think UFO's have natural causes, even though scientists cannot explain all UFO reports. Observers have described various kinds of UFO's. Many of these objects resemble a glowing tube or saucer and fly silently at high speeds, displaying manoeuvres that would be unusual for an aircraft of any kind. UFO's have been reported to have frightened animals, caused static on radios, and landed and left marks on the ground.

Scientists have tried to provide logical explanations for most UFO reports. For example, in many cases, a reported UFO later was identified as a meteor, a planet, a rocket, a star, an artificial satellite, or a weather balloon. Aircraft or their exhaust trails, seen under unusual lighting conditions, have also been reported as UFO's. In addition, atmospheric conditions may produce optical illusions that are described as UFO's.

From 1966 to 1968, a major study of UFO's took place in the United States. The U.S. Air Force sponsored the study, by scientists at the University of Colorado. The scientists could not explain all the UFO reports.

Researchers generally mark the beginning of the UFO phenomenon as the sighting of dirigible-like "mystery ships" over the United States in 1896-97. The next significant group of reports came during World War II, from both Allied and Axis pilots. The pilots reported seeing strange metal-like objects, which they called "foo fighters," in controlled flight around their planes. In 1946 people in Europe, particularly Scandinavia, reported large-scale sightings of silent "ghost rockets." None of these phenomena has been satisfactorily explained.

The UFO phenomenon entered public consciousness on June 24, 1947, when American pilot Kenneth Arnold reported sighting nine circular objects flying across his airplane's path in the skies over the state of Washington. His description of their movements as being like "saucers skipping over the water" gave birth to the term "flying saucer." Such shapes have often been reported since that time. Objects shaped like cigars, squares, balls, triangles, rings, and hats are also reported, as are amorphous and shape-changing objects. The sightings have taken place in nearly every country.

Occasionally the number of UFO sightings increases rapidly. For instance, waves of sightings occurred in France and Italy in 1954, in New Guinea in 1958, and in the USSR in 1967. In the United States, waves have occurred in every decade. UFO researchers have not been able to predict or explain these waves.

A study of reports suggests that UFO sightings are random. The witnesses cannot be usefully categorized. Instead they cut across economic, class, racial, and educational lines. A greater percentage of reports, however, have come from people living in rural areas than from those living in urban areas. The reasons for this disparity are unknown.

UFO Encounters Classification

Dr. J. Allen Hynek devised a classification system for close encounters. These categories have been widely accepted by ufologists and they stand to this day.

Close Encounters of the First Kind (Ce1)
The appearance of a UFO within 500 feet or less of the witness.

Close Encounters of the Second Kind (Ce2)
Incidents in which a UFO affects the environment in some way, for example by scorching vegetation, leaving landing traces, burning or otherwise injuring witnesses. The UFO has a measurable physical effect on either animate or inanimate matter.

Close Encounters of the Third Kind (Ce3)
Reports of beings, usually humanoid, in connection with UFO sightings. One subset of CE3s is the Abduction Experience, in which persons allegedly are taken against their will into UFOs and subjected by their humanoid occupants to physical tests or experiments before they are released, usually with memory impairment. Memory may return under hypnotic regression or spontaneous recall.

Close Encounters of the Fourth Kind (Ce4)
Abduction by an alien. Abductee's experience severe reality distortion such as memory lapse, 'post abduction trauma' symptoms such as fear and anxiety.

Close Encounters of the Fifth Kind (Ce5)
Communication between a human being and an extra-terrestrial.

Lt. Gorman's Dogfight

Full Report/Article

One of the early "classics" of UFO history involved Lieutenant George F. Gorman of the North Dakota Air National Guard, who said he had a twenty-seven minute "dogfight" with a UFO in the skies above Fargo.

Date October 1, 1948
Location Fargo, North Dakota, United States

Gorman, then manager of a Fargo construction company, told this story to Air Force investigators:

On the night of October 1, 1948, he had been on a cross-country flight with his squadron. Upon return to Hector airport in Fargo, he elected to log some night flying time, so he remained airborne after the other planes had landed. He had circled his F-51 over the lighted football stadium and around the city and was preparing to land about 9 P.M. The control tower cleared him to land, advising him about a Piper Cub in the vicinity - the only other plane - and he could see the light aircraft outlined plainly about 500 feet below him. What appeared to be the taillight of a plane passed him on the right, but the tower insisted they knew of no other planes in the area.

Gorman informed the tower that he was going to investigate the other aircraft and pulled his F-51 up and out toward the moving light. He closed to within about 1,000 yards and took a good look at the object.

"It was about six to eight inches in diameter, clear white, and completely round without fuzz at the edges [i.e., sharp and clear]. It was blinking on and off. As I approached, however, the light suddenly became steady and pulled into a sharp left bank. I thought it was making a pass at the tower. I dived after it and brought my manifold pressure up to sixty inches but I couldn't catch up with the thing. It started gaining altitude and again made a left bank, I put my F-51 into a sharp turn and tried to cut the light off in its turn. By then we were at about 7,000 feet. Suddenly it made a sharp right turn and we headed straight at each other. Just when we were about to collide, I guess I got scared. I went into a dive and the light passed over my canopy at about 500 feet. Then, it made a left circle about 1,000 feet above, and I gave chase again."

Gorman said he cut sharply toward the light, which was once more coming at him. When collision again seemed imminent, the object shot straight up into the air in a steep climb-out, disappearing overhead. Gorman again attempted to pursue it but his plane went into a power stall at about 14,000 feet, and the object was not seen again. It was then 9:27 P.M.

Gorman was so shaken by the encounter that he had difficulty handling his plane, although he was a veteran pilot and a flying instructor during World War II. He had noticed no sound, odour, or exhaust trail from the object during the "dogfight," and no deviation on his instruments. At times during the chase, he had pushed the F-51 to full power, sometimes reaching 400 m.p.h.. He described the object as round and somewhat flattened.

In the airport control tower, traffic controllers Lloyd D. Jensen and H. E. Johnson also saw a strange light near the airfield:

"After passing to the east of the airport it seemed to take a northwest heading, The object seemed to be at about 2,000 feet and appeared to be travelling at quite an a high speed compared to a Piper Cub that was east of the field at the time. No definite outline could be identified. Both objects [the UFO and the Piper Cub] were sighted at the same time." Jensen said that through binoculars he sighted,

"An object or a light travelling at a high rate of speed, apparently on a southwest heading. The F-51 [Gorman's plane] was some distance behind and the object was travelling fast enough to increase the spacing between itself and the fighter. The object appeared to be only a round light, perfectly formed, with no fuzzy edges or rays leaving its body. The edges were clear cut. No other shape was observed. The main identifying characteristic was the high rate of speed at which it was apparently travelling." The pilot of the Piper Cub, Dr. A. E. Cannon, and his passenger, Einar Nielson, also witnessed the swiftly moving light while in radio communication with the tower:

"While circling the football field at NDAC at 1,600 feet, Fargo tower advised us that there was an F-51 in the air and a few moments later asked us who the third plane might be,"

Cannon said, "We had noticed the 51 and when we were over the north side of Hector field going west, a light, seemingly on a plane, passed above and to the north, moving very swiftly toward the west. At first we thought it was the 51, but we then saw the light of the 51 higher and move over the field. We landed on Runway 3, taxied to the administration building, and went up to the tower and listened to the calls from the 51, which seemed to be trying to overtake the plane or lighted object, which then went southwest and over the city. The object was moving very swiftly, much faster than the 51. We tried to get a better view with a pair of binoculars, but couldn't follow it well enough."

In a statement to Major D. C. Jones, commander of the 17th Fighter Squadron at Hector airport, Gorman said he was convinced that there was "thought" behind the manoeuvres:

"I am also convinced that the object was governed by the laws of inertia because its acceleration was rapid but not immediate, and although it was able to turn fairly tight at considerable speed, it still followed a natural curve."

The object could outturn and outspeed the F-51, he said, and was able to attain a much steeper climb and to maintain a constant rate of climb far in excess of the F-51.

"When I attempted to turn with the object, I blacked out temporarily due to excessive speed," Gorman stated. "I am in fairly good physical condition and I do not believe there are many, if any, pilots who could withstand the turn effected by the light and remain conscious."

George F. Gorman retired from the Air Force in 1969 with the rank of Lieutenant Colonel and was then living in Texas.

Kenneth Arnold Sighting

Full Report/Article

On June 24, 1947, Kenneth Arnold saw something that would change his life forever. His experience also served as a catalyst for our modern UFO craze.

Date June 24, 1947
Location Yakima, Washington, United States

Arnold, a recreational private pilot, was returning home from a flight in Wyoming when he received a radio signal requesting assistance in the Yakima, Washington area. It seems there was a missing troop transport and a aerial search party was being assembled.

At 3:00 P.M., flying at 9,000 feet, a bright flash of light caught Arnold's attention. Turning to look out of the side window of his airplane, Arnold was amazed to see nine saucer shaped objects flying in formation. Thinking they were some sort of military aircraft, he watched them intently as they bobbed, weaved, and darted about flying at an amazingly high rate of speed. What fascinated Arnold the most was the fact that the flying objects had no tail, but rather were round, saucer shaped, metallic and highly polished.

Arnold radioed in his sighting and the uproar began. When he landed he was surprised to find a news conference scheduled at the Pendleton field in Oregon. It was at this news conference that Arnold gave the world the first description of a saucer shaped object. The term 'flying saucers' was coined and the UFO craze began.

The Death of Thomas Mantell

Full Report/Article

January 7, 1948, would be a day of tragedy for Captain Thomas F. Mantell of the Kentucky Air National Guard, and his family, friends, and fellow Guardsmen. The Mandell case will forever be an important part of the hotbed of UFO reports of the late 1940s and early 1950s. He would have the unfortunate distinction of being the first human being to give his life in the ongoing chase for the elusive truth behind bizarre reports of flying craft from other worlds. Was

Date January 7, 1948
Location Standiford AFB, Kentucy, United States

his sighting a carry-over from the foo-fighters of World War II? or were they altogether another phenomena a phenomena that was just out of his reach? He gave all he had to reach this mysterious, intelligently controlled metallic craft, but whatever it was, and whoever controlled it, escaped that day...the day Thomas Mantell lost his life.

Mantell was piloting an F-51 that fateful day, soaring to Standiford Air Force Base, Kentucky. He was accompanied by three other Guard planes. At approximately 1:30 P.M. the Kentucky State Police began receiving reports from worried citizens of spotting a large circular object flying over the city of Mansville. In a matter of minutes the area of the sightings expanded to cover Irvington and Owensboro. This large, metallic flying craft was then clearly seen from the tower of Godman Air Force Base. The object was described as being an extremely large, round, whitish in colour, with a red light toward it's bottom side, and seemed to be moving slowly toward the South. A little over an hour after the first reports, Mantell and his crew were asked to investigate the anomalous object.

The actual transcripts read;

"Godman Tower Calling the flight of 4 ships northbound over Godman Field. Do you read? Over.

[Pause] Godman Tower Calling the flight of 4 ships northbound over Godman Field. Do you read? Over."

"Roger, Godman Tower. This is National Guard 869, Flight Leader of the formation. Over."

"National Guard 869 from Godman Tower. We have an object out south of Godman here that we are unable to identify, and we would like to know if you have gas enough; and if so could you take a look for us if you will."

"Roger, I have the gas and I will take a look for you if you give me the correct heading.

One of his three companions in flight received permission to continue his pre-assigned flight plan, while Mantell and the remaining two planes headed to the coordinates of the visual sightings.

Mantell led the way in the climb to 15,000 feet, and upon reaching the position, he radioed the following statement back to the control tower.

"The object is directly ahead of and above me now, moving at about half my speed...It appears to be a metallic object or possibly reflection of Sun from a metallic object, and it is of tremendous size...I'm still climbing... I'm trying to close in for a better look."

18,000, 20,000, 22,000 feet! too high for the WWII fighters without oxygen! The other two planes turned back, leaving Mantell alone to pursue the giant object. By all accounts Mantell must have passed out from lack of oxygen at about 30,000; at least his plane leveled off at that height. His plane now began to plunge back toward earth. He crashed a few harrowing moments later on the farm of William J. Phillips near Franklin, Kentucky. Mantell's watch stopped at 3:16 P.M., and his body was still strapped in his plane, which become his coffin. He had spent 45 minutes in a frantic flight into the realm of the unknown. By 3:50 P.M., the giant craft was not visible from Godman, but reports continued as the UFO continued southward into Tennessee.

The reports of the incident spread like wildfire. Theory and speculation reached radio shows, television, and newspapers. The New York Times' story began with this headline, "Flier Dies Chasing A `Flying Saucer," and another story was headlined with, "Plane Exploded Over Kentucky as That and Near States Report Strange Object." Common speculation that Mantell was chasing a UFO was countered by the Air Force, which initially concluded that Mantell and his co-pilots were chasing the planet Venus. They also announced that his death was directly related to oxygen deprivation.

This almost comical conclusion was hastily put to rest by an eye witness, Glen Mays, who lived near Franklin. Mays stated categorically that Mantell's plane exploded in mid-air."

The plane circled three times, like the pilot didn't know where he was going," reported Mays, "and then started down into a dive from about 20,000 feet. About halfway down there was a terrific explosion."

Also, there is the testimony of Godman Base Commander Guy F. Hix, who stated to reporters that he observed the craft for almost an hour through binoculars. He would not have confused what he saw with the planet Venus.

Richard T. Miller, who was in the Operations Room of Scott Air Force Base in Belleville, Illinois also made several profound statements regarding the crash. He was monitoring the radio talk between Mantell and Godman tower, and heard this statement very clearly.

"My God, I see people in this thing!"

Miller added that on the morning after the crash, at a briefing, investigators had stated that Mantell died "pursuing an intelligently controlled unidentified flying object."

In conclusion, Miller made this statement, "that evening, Air Technical Intelligence Centre officers from Wright-Patterson AFB arrived and ordered all personnel to turn over any materials relating to the crash. Then, after we had turned it over to them, they said they had already completed the investigation. I was no longer a skeptic. I had been up to that time. Now I wondered why the Government had gone to all of the trouble of covering it up, to keep it away from the press and the public."

In recent years, additional information has come forward. Captain James F. Duesler, who was one of several military officers at Godman, was retired and living in England. In 1997, he stated that he and several other officers actually saw the gigantic UFO hovering over Godman field that day. Duesler, who was a pilot and crash investigator, stated, "the UFO was a strange gray-looking object, which looked like a rotating inverted ice cream cone."

Shortly after the crash, Duesler visited the site, and made these observations, "The wings and tail section had broken off on impact with the ground and were a short distance from the plane," he recalled. "There was no damage to the surrounding trees and it was obvious that there had been no forward or sideways motion when the plane had come down. It just appeared to have "belly flopped" into the clearing. There was very little damage to the fuselage, which was in one piece, and no signs of blood whatsoever in the cockpit. There was no scratching on the body of the fuselage to indicate any forward movement and the propeller blade bore no telltale scratch marks to show it had been rotating at the time of impact, and one blade had been embedded into the ground. The damage pattern was not consistent with an aircraft of this type crashing at high speed into the ground. Because of the large engine in the nose of the plane, it would come down nose first and hit the ground at an angle. Even if it had managed to glide in, it would have cut a swath through the trees and a channel into the ground. None of these signs were present. All indications were that it had just belly flopped into the clearing. I must admit, I found this very strange."

To further debunk the "Venus" theory, astronomical records indicated that the planet was only 33 degrees above the horizon at the time of the incident, thus totally eliminating it from the case.

The Air Force, embarrassed by the "Venus" theory falling through, now searched for another "wordly" explanation for the object observed that day. After discovering that Naval research was sending up the enormous "Skyhook" balloons, the Air Force had their alternate solution. This theory was also soon aborted after discovering that no balloon was launched, or could have been in the skies that day. The UFO theory received even more credence after Mantell's death. On January 8, residents of Clinton, North Carolina, reported a cone-shaped object moving through the skies at incredible speeds, and on February 1, a large metallic UFO was seen emitting an orange light near the ground at Circleville, Ohio. Whatever happened on the day that Thomas Mantell crashed his plane, it is certain that it was not a weather balloon, and it was not Venus, or any other planet. Could it have been a visitor from another planet, or another dimension?

The Chiles/Whitted Sighting

Full Report/Article

A classic UFO event that has all but been forgotten is the Chiles-Whitted sighting which unfolded over Montgomery, Alabama on July 24, 1948. This case was one of the very first reports of a large UFO officially made by commercial airplane pilots. The experience was a one of a kind for the two seasoned pilots, Captain Clarence S. Chiles, and co-pilot John B. Whitted. While flying an Eastern Airlines DC-3 from Houston, Texas to Atlanta, Georgia they encountered a huge cigar-shaped UFO which barely missed them. This extraordinary event transpired while the DC-3 was cruising 5,000 feet above the city of Montgomery, Alabama.

Date July 24, 1948
Location Montgomery, Alabama, United States

The first part of their journey was a pleasant, uneventful one until 2:45 A.M. Their relaxed cruising mode was suddenly interrupted by the sight of what seemed to be a dullish-red glowing object, directly in their flight path. Still at a distance, the two pilots first impression was that they were looking at a jet, unreported, and coming right at them! The glowing object barely missed them, passing on their starboard side at a distance of about 1,000 feet, according to Chiles. Whitted would later estimate the distance at somewhat more than Chiles' guess.

The two pilots both agreed that the object had no wings or tail section. Both also agreed seeing at least two rows of windows from which appeared a glowing like "burning magnesium." The object had a pointed nose section, and there was a "bluish glow" running on it's belly from nose to it's end. Out of it's rear end, an "orange-red" exhaust was seen by the two unnerved crewmen. This so-called emission was as long again as the object's body. Both pilots were also in agreement that the object's length was approximately that of a B-29 bomber, though somewhat thicker.

Captain Chiles' first reaction was to turn his DC-3 off to the left, as the object seemed to be coming slightly to his right. Both pilots clearly witnessed the oncoming craft do an abrupt pull-up, just after missing them. Only Whitted was able to view the object as it seemed to momentarily disappear after making a rapid vertical ascent. When asked later to elaborate on his description, he added, "the object vanished instantaneously after its sharp pull-up." The unusual object and it's dash at the DC-3 was fully reported to Eastern officials and Project Sign.

Some further details were made available in this report. The two pilots stated that "no disturbance was felt from airwaves, nor was there any wash or mechanical disturbance when the object passed." Other witnesses would later disagree with this statement, and in the Naval Intelligence Report of the incident, it is stated by at least one of the passengers that the "DC-3 was rocked by the wash from the object." Witnesses also describe a sound like that of a V-2 rocket. Most of the passengers were, fortunately for them, asleep at the time of the occurrence. Clarence McKelvie, who was assistant editor of the American Education Press at Columbus, Ohio stated, "I saw no shape or form. It was on the right side of the plane, and suddenly I saw this strange, eerie streak out of my window. It was very intense, not like lightning or anything I had ever seen before."

Chiles, Whitted, and McKelvie were not the only observers of this strange sight that morning. Several witnesses from Robbins

Air Base, near Macon, Georgia stated they saw an object of the same description about 1/2 hour before the DC-3 sighting. The object was reported as travelling in a southerly direction at a high rate of speed. An official government investigation ruled out the possibility of a conventional aircraft after tracing flight records of 225 civilian and military flights that morning. Private debunkers, with no consideration of the facts, wrote the sighting off as an illusion due to temperature inversions, and then later assigned the sighting to a meteor. Project Sign would agree on the meteor theory, but in usual fashion, added that the description of the object and it's manoeuvres did not match that of a meteor. This near-collision is still listed under the "unexplained" category.

The Lubbock Lights

Full Report/Article
Source

At 9:10 P.M. on August 25, 1951, Dr. W. I. Robinson, professor of geology at the Texas technological College, stood in the back yard of his home in Lubbock, Texas and chatted with two colleagues. The other men were Dr. A. G. Oberg, a professor of chemical engineering, and Professor W. L. Ducker, head of the department of petroleum engineering. The night was clear and dark. Suddenly all three men saw a number of lights race noiselessly across the sky, from horizon to horizon, in a few seconds. They gave the impression of about

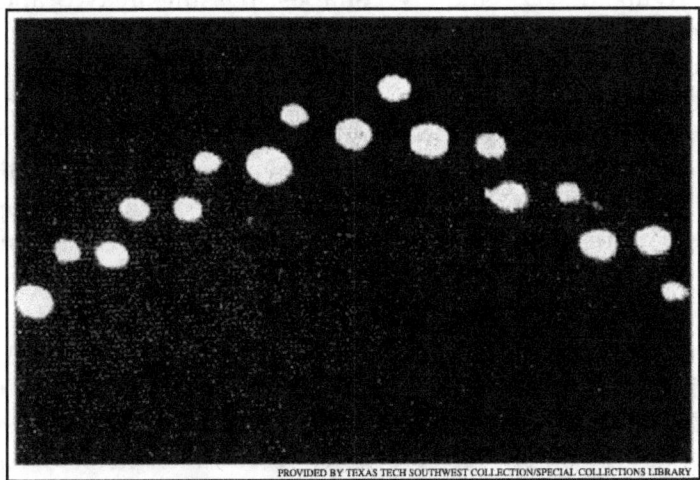

PROVIDED BY TEXAS TECH SOUTHWEST COLLECTION/SPECIAL COLLECTIONS LIBRARY

Date August 25, 1951
Location Lubbock, Texas, United States

30 luminous beads, arranged in a crescent shape. A few moments later another similar formation flashed across the night. This time the scientists were able to judge that the lights moved through 30 degrees of arc in a second. A check the next day with the Air Force showed that no planes had been over the area at the time. This was but the beginning: Professor Ducker observed 12 flights of the luminous objects between August and November of last year. Some of his colleagues observed as many as 10. Hundreds of nonscientific observers in a wide vicinity around Lubbock have seen as many as three flights of the mysterious crescents in one night.

On the night of August 30 an attempt to photograph the lights was made by 18-year old Carl Hart Jr. He used a Kodak 35-mm camera at f3.5, 1/10 of a second. Working rapidly, Hart managed to get five exposures of the flights. The pictures exhibited by Hart as the result of this effort show 18 to 20 luminous objects, more intense than the planet Venus, arranged in one or a pair of crescents. In several photographs, off to one side of the main flight, a larger luminosity is visible –like a mother craft hovering near its aerial brood.

It seemed an ordinary Lubbock night when ... The first sightings began on the night of August 25 at 9:20 P.M. and continued for the next several evenings. Witnesses said they saw "dots" of lights flying in "U" and "V" shapes, passing in two and three-second intervals. The number of dots reported in the formations ranged from eight to nine to 20 to 30. The lights appeared in the northeastern part of the sky and proceeded in a straight line to the southwest. The colour of the lights were "about like the stars, only brighter," while others said they were either a blue or white with a slight yellow tinge to them. Others described them as appearing "as a string of beads," moving roughly in a semi-circle, and were "soft, glowing, bluish-green."

Another group of lights came over three minutes after the first group had been sighted. Officials at Reese Air Force Base and the Civil Aeronautics Administration both reported that to their knowledge, there were no jet planes flying in the area on the nights of the sightings. The photographs were taken at 5:30 P.M. and 10:37 P.M. The three Texas tech professors examined the 18-year-old's photographs, but could find no explanation for the photos. Witness Roger Dods heard a slight rustling or whooshing sound as the objects passed over head. He reported seeing them at 10:37 P.M. In late September, a report on the Lubbock Lights reached the Air Force. The Air Force examined the pictures in great detail and could neither prove nor disprove their authenticity. Captain Edward J. Ruppelt, the Air Force officer who became the first director of Project Blue Book, travelled to Lubbock to investigate the case. Ruppelt later wrote a very good book about his experiences as a UFO investigator, called "The Report on Unidentified Flying Objects."

It was Ruppelt who interviewed an elderly rancher in Brownfield. The rancher claimed to have heard the "unmistakable call of the plover," a water bird with a one-foot wingspread and an oily white breast that "could easily reflect city lights." But game wardens said that the phenomenon could not have been plovers (birds about the size of a quail) since these birds never fly in flocks larger than three. T.E. Snyder, Jr. reported, "I saw something like people have been seeing and it definitely was ducks." Although not accounting for the unbelievable speed, a reflection from the Westerner drive-in theater caused some ducks to be illuminated. Everything seemed to point to flights of birds as the explanation of the mysterious phenomenon that came to be known as the "Lubbock Lights," and yet there are those who disagree.

Dr. J.C. Cross, head of Tech's Department of Biology, examined the 35mm photographs, and asserted, "It definitely wasn't caused by birds." In Matador, reports were made of a "noiseless aircraft flying at a low altitude, without aid of propellers or wings." They said it was different from any aircraft they had ever seen.

To this day, there are those who contend that Lubbock was visited by UFOs, while others say that it was merely a natural phenomenon. No one really can say for sure, but as is stated the History of Lubbock, "Lubbock's reputation is greater in scientific circles for the Lubbock Light Sightings (and flying saucers) than for any economic or civic reason." So on these warm August nights, as one stares into the West Texas skies, they can look at the lights that glisten in the distance, and ponder the legend of the Lubbock Lights.

The Fort Monmouth UFO Case

Full Report/Article

The Fort Monmouth Case began with a watershed event which took place at 11:18 A.M. EDT on a clear morning in September 1951. It was Monday the 10th. The place was a radar facility near the coastline at Fort Monmouth, New Jersey. A young student Army Signal Corps radar operator, PFC Eugent A. Clark, had just picked up an unknown low-flying target moving faster than the automatic setting mode on his AN/MPG-1 radar set could plot.

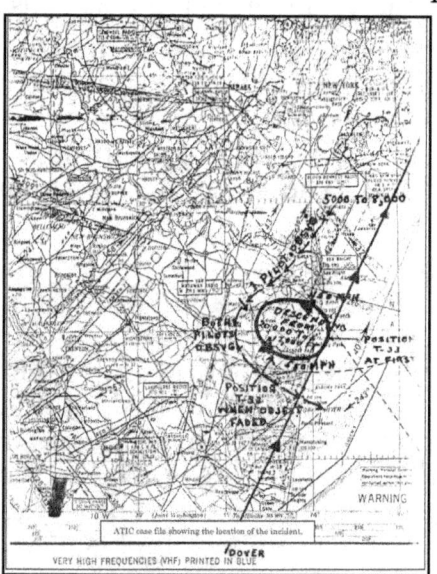

Date September 10, 1951
Location Fort Monmouth, New Jersey, United States

As a matter of coincidence, a number of visiting Army officers happened to be standing behind Clark at the time, witnessing the strange event unfold. They watched in amazement as in just moments the curious radar blip traversed the coast line at an estimated speed of at least 700 miles per hour. It was lost off the scope near the Sandy Hook coastal peninsula, not far from south of New York City.

This radar tracking caused a lot of excitement. In 1951, although jets had reached such speeds in special tests, they flew nowhere near those velocities on a routine or even sustained basis.

Seventeen minutes later, the story became even more bizarre. Just south of Sandy Hook, at 11:35 A.M. EDT, a T-33 jet trainer piloted by Lieutenant Wilbert S. Rogers, with Major Edward Ballard Jr. in the rear seat, encountered a completely unrecognizable object. They were flying northward at 20,000 feet over Point Pleasant, New Jersey headed toward Sandy Hook. At that moment Rogers spotted off to his left a dull, silvery object passing far below on an opposing parallel course. It was southward bound from the coastline peninsula of Sandy Hook and appeared to be about 12,000 feet below them. Rogers had been on a direct pre-approach heading toward a landing into Mitchel AFB, New York, but wanted Major Ballard to have a look at it. Ballard, however, was on the radio so Rogers turned slightly to the left to linger and waited for him to complete his radio communication. Forty-five seconds later Ballard had caught sight of it, by which time the UFO entered a descending arc-like turn that was about to cut under their flight path. At that moment the pilots' conversations were heard by ground control via an open mike.

Records show the pilots were excited as both men were watching the object bank. As it did, it revealed a 'discus-like' silhouette while continuing its turn. So Rogers kept turning left with it to keep it from going under his wing and thus out of view. While the object proceeded to descend further, Rogers nosed his jet down to eventually complete a hair raising 360-degree, 3,000 feet descending manoeuvre, just to keep it in sight.

Both Rogers and Ballard estimated the craft to be around 30 to 50 feet in diameter and perhaps moving as fast as 700 miles per hour. By then the pilots knew that they were definitely not chasing a balloon because this thing was not only banking left but was by then out-pacing their jet which Rogers had throttled up from 450 to 550 miles per hour! By that point the object had completed a 90 degree turn and was heading away from the coastline, travelling out over the ocean in level flight near the speed of sound at around 5,000 feet. Rogers vainly attempted to parallel its course from his current altitude of 17,000 feet as the UFO continued to increase its speed out to sea, covering 35 miles during the short two minute span of the sighting.

Rogers, an experienced WWII fighter pilot, was later asked by a reporter what he thought it was that they had seen that day. He shrugged and only said that the object was something he had never seen before in his life, and it certainly wasn't a balloon because it was not only descending but moving at great speed. He added that the object looked perfectly round and flat with the centre of the object being somewhat raised.

Operation Mainbrace Sightings

Full Report/Article

In the vicinity of Denmark and Norway. September, 1952. A particularly interesting series of UFO reports came from the vicinity of the "Operation Mainbrace" NATO manoeuvres held in September 1952. The manoeuvres commenced September 13th and lasted twelve days. According to the U. S. Navy, "units of eight NATO governments and New Zealand participated, including 80,000 men, 1,000 planes, and 200 ships . . . in the vicinity of Denmark and Norway . . . ." Directed by British Admiral Sir Patrick Brind, "it was the largest NATO manoeuvre held up until that time."

Date September 19-28, 1952
Location Denmark and Norway

September 13--The Danish destroyer Willemoes, participating in the manoeuvres, was north of Bornholm Island. During the night, Lieutenant Commander Schmidt Jensen and several members of the crew saw an unidentified object, triangular in shape, which moved at high speed toward the southeast. The object emitted a bluish glow. Commander Jensen estimated the speed at over 900 m.p.h..

Within the next week, there were four important sightings by well-qualified observers. (Various sources differ by a day or two on the exact dates, but agree on details. There is no question about the authenticity of the sightings; the British cases were officially reported by the Air Ministry, the others are confirmed by reliable witnesses. All occurred on or about September 20).

September 19--A British Meteor jet aircraft was returning to the airfield at Topcliffe, Yorkshire, England, just before 11 A.M. As it approached for landing, a silvery object was observed following it, swaying back and forth like a pendulum. Lieutenant John W. Kilburn and other observers on the ground said that when the Meteor began circling, the UFO stopped. It was disk-shaped, and rotated on its axis while hovering. The disk suddenly took off westward at high speed, changed course, and disappeared to the southeast.

About September 20--Personnel of the U.S.S. Franklin D. Roosevelt, an aircraft carrier participating in the Mainbrace manoeuvres, observed a silvery, spherical object which was also photographed. (The pictures have never been made public). The UFO was seen moving across the sky behind the fleet. Reporter Wallace Litwin took a series of colour photographs, which were examined by Navy Intelligence officers. The Air Force project chief, Captain Ruppelt stated: "[The pictures] turned out to be excellent . . . . judging by the size of the object in each successive photo, one could see that is was moving rapidly." The possibility that a balloon had been launched from one of the ships was immediately checked out. No unit had launched a balloon. A poor print of one of the photographs appears in the Project Blue Book files, but with no analysis report.

September 20--At Karup Field, Denmark, three Danish Air Force officers sighted a UFO about 7:30 P.M. The object, a shiny disk with metallic appearance, passed overhead from the direction of the fleet and disappeared in clouds to the east.

September 21--Six British pilots flying a formation of RAF jets above the North Sea observed a shiny sphere approaching from the direction of the fleet. The UFO eluded their pursuit and disappeared. When returning to base, one of the pilots looked back and saw the UFO following him. He turned to chase it, but the UFO also turned and sped away.

September 27/28--Throughout Western Germany, Denmark, and southern Sweden, there were widespread UFO reports. A brightly luminous object with a cometlike tail was visible for a long period of time moving irregularly near Hamburg and Kiel. On one occasion, three satellite objects were reported moving around a larger object. A cigar-shaped object moving silently eastward also was reported.

Since existing documentation shows that U. S. Navy and Air Force Intelligence, and the RAF, were studying these incidents, it is a safe assumption that more information exists in the files of NATO, the British Air Ministry, the U. S. Navy, and the U. S. Air Force. The sightings remain unexplained.

B-29 Crew Encounters UFOs

Full Report/Article

In December 1952 Lieutenant Sid Coleman was Radar Officer aboard a B-29 bomber near Galveston. When watching the radar scope Coleman observed two UFOs which he tracked at a speed in excess of 5,000 miles per hour, quite impossible for planes of the day. The captain of the plane, John Harta, suggested that Coleman recalibrate his set as the sighting was impossible but the sighting was immediately confirmed by the navigator on his radar scope. Eventually four UFOs were seen on the radar screen.

Date December, 1952
Location Galveston, Texas, United States

From the plane, they were also able to make visual contact with the object, watching it as a blue-white streak moving fast near the bomber. Shortly after this there was a repeat with several more objects whizzing past their plane. Crew members watched the UFOs perform incredible manoeuvres to avoid hitting the plane. There were reports of a mothercraft absorbing smaller craft and one report of one UFO moving at over 9,000 miles per hour.

The Sea Fury Incident

Full Report/Article

One of the most controversial radar visual reports of the fifties occurred on August 31, 1954. The story leaked out in December 1954, and made front page headlines. The official navy file on the event remained classified until the Directorate of Naval Intelligence released a copy in 1982. During his 1973 visit to Australia, Dr. Hynek was able to interview the pilot involved in this famous incident, which became known as the "Sea Fury" encounter.

Date August 31, 1954
Location Nowra, Australia

Lieutenant J.A. O'Farrell was returning to Royal Australian Navy Air Station Nowra after a night cross country in a Sea Fury aircraft. After contacting Nowra at about 1910 hours, O'Farrell saw a very bright light closing fast at one o'clock. It crossed in front of his aircraft taking up position on his port beam, where it appeared to orbit. A second and similar light was observed at nine o'clock. It passed about a mile in from of the Sea Fury and then turned in the position where the first light was observed.

According to O'Farrell, the apparent crossing speeds of the lights were the fastest he had ever encountered. He had been flying at 220 knots. O'Farrell contacted Nowra who in turn confirmed that they had two radar "paints" in company with him. The radar operator, Petty Officer Keith Jessop, confirmed the presence of two objects near the Sea Fury on the G.C.I. remote display. The two lights reformed at nine o'clock and then disappeared on a north easterly heading. O'Farrell could only make out "a vague shape with the white light situated centrally on top."

The Directorate of Naval Intelligence at the time wrote that O'Farrell was "an entirely credible witness" and that he "was visibly 'shaken' by his experience, but remains adamant that he saw these objects"

In a recent interview, "Shamus" O'Farrell described the incident:

"I said, "Nowra, this is 921. Do you have me on radar." "And a few seconds later they came back and said, "Affirmative 921. We have you coming in from the west. We have another two contacts as well. Which one are you." "I said, "I think I'm the central one." And so they said, "Do a 180...for identification." So I did a quick 180 and then continued on around and made it a 360 back to where I was going.

"They said, "Yes, we've got you. You're the centre aircraft." I said that's correct. They then said to me, "Who are the other two aircraft," and I said, "I don't know. I was hoping you would tell me, because I didn't think there was anyone up here. "They said, "Well there shouldn't be, and they certainly shouldn't be that close to you."

"So the conversation went on like this and I was very pleased to be talking to somebody because it gave me a lot of reassurance. With that these two aircraft came in quite close to me and I could really see the dark mass and that they were quite big, but I couldn't make out any other lights or any other form of an aircraft. With that they took off and headed off to the north east at great speed.

"I was about to press the button and tell them at Nowra that the two aircraft were departing when Nowra called me up and said, "The other two aircraft appear to be departing at high speed to the north east. Is that correct?" and I said, "Yes!". And they said, "Roger, we'll see if we can track them." They tracked them for a while and then lost them. "I came in and landed at 7.30 (19:30) and when I got there there were quite a few people waiting for me. I thought it was a bit strange and so they came over, and they said, "You sure you had aircraft out there!", and I said yes.

The Surgeon Commander came over and spoke to me. He said did I feel sick, or was I upset. I said no. He ran his hand over my head to see whether I had any bumps. He had a look at me and decided I was okay. So then he said, "Perhaps you'd like to come to the sick bay after you've changed and we'll do an examination." So after I was finished I went up to sick bay and he gave me a more thorough medical, and said, no, I appeared to be alright. I found out later, that at the same time, they checked to make sure I hadn't been drinking before I took off and all that sort of thing."

During this interview, Dr. Hynek's involvement came up:

"This man (Hynek) - a professor - had made a study of thousands of sightings all around the world and he had decided my sighting was one of those that he had not been able to explain away by other means. Any way I had a talk with him. He was a very interesting chap and he made the comment that there were about 13 or 15, I don't remember, sightings that he was aware of over the years that were like mine and could not be explained away. The interesting thing he said was that all of these sightings had been made by professional people in aviation.

By that he meant they were military pilots, military air crew, civil aviation operators, air traffic controllers, and the like, or airline pilots. These were the ones he was now (1973) going around meeting the people themselves and investigating. All the others he had written off and had been able to explain down to some other phenomena. It came to the point where he said, "Your sighting cannot be explained away." And he left it at that. To this day I wouldn't know where it came from or where it went."

US Senators see Flying Saucers in Soviet Russia

Full Report/Article
One of the most powerful U.S. senators in modern history actually eye-witnessed two UFO's while on a fact-finding trip through Russia in 1955 and the U.S. government kept the sightings a secret for more than three decades. The incredible encounter is detailed in 12 TOP SECRET CIA, FBI, and Air Force reports and declassified in 1985. Those startling reports reveal that Senator Richard B. Russell, Jr. (D-GA)-then chairman of the Armed Services Committee was on a Soviet train when he spotted a disc-shaped craft taking off near the tracks. He hurriedly called his military aide and interpreter to the window and they saw the UFO, plus another one that appeared a minute later. The astonished trio reported the sightings to the U.S. Air Force as soon as they were out of Russia.

Date October 4, 1955
Location Transcaucasus region, Russia

"The three observers were firmly convinced that they saw a genuine flying disc," says an Air Force Intelligence report, dated October 14, 1955, and classified TOP SECRET at the time. Senator Russell served 38 years in the Senate. He was its senior, and one of the most influential, senators at the time of his death in 1971. He was chairman of the Armed Services Committee from 1951 to 1969, and unsuccessfully sought the Democratic Presidential nomination in 1952. The mind-boggling documents detailing his UFO encounter were made available by the Fund for UFO Research and its chairman, Dr. Bruce Maccabee. Several key documents were obtained by the group through the Freedom of Information Act. "These long secret documents are of major importance because they show for the first time that one of the most powerful U.S. Senators witnessed and reported a UFO," said Dr. Maccabee.

The Air Force Intelligence report says Russell and his two traveling companions spotted the UFO's on October 4, 1955, while travelling by rail across Russia's Transcaucasus region. "One disc ascended almost vertically, at a relatively slow speed, with its outer surface revolving slowly to the right, to an altitude of about 6000 feet, where its speed then increased sharply as it headed north," the report states. "The second flying disc was seen performing the same actions about one minute later. The take-off area was about 1-2 miles south of the rail line.

" Russell" saw the first flying disc ascend and pass over the train," and went "rushing in to get Mr Efron (Ruben Efron, his interpreter) and Col. Hathaway (Col. E. U. Hathaway, his aide) to see it," the report said. "Col. Hathaway stated that he got to the window with the Senator in time to see the first (UFO), while Mr. Efron said that he got only a short glimpse of the first. However, all three saw the second disc and all agreed that they saw the same round, disc-shaped crafts the first." The Air Force report was written by Lieut. Col. Thomas Ryan, who interviewed Senator Russell's companions in Prague, Czechoslovakia, on October 13, after they arrived there from Russia shortly after the sighting.

In his report, Col. Ryan called the sightings "an eyewitness account of the ascent and flight of an unconventional craft by three highly reliable United States observers. He added that Col. Hathaway led off his account of the sightings by saying: "I doubt if your going to believe this, but we all saw it. Senator Russell was the first to see this flying disc we've been told for years that there isn't such a thing, but all of us saw it."

CIA documents show that the agency later interviewed the three eyewitnesses in the Russell party and also a fourth person, unidentified in the reports, who had seen the UFO's. An eyewitness whose name was blacked out on the CIA report prior to its declassification said one of the UFO's "had a slight dome on top" and also a "white light on top." The edge of the disc was glowing pinkish-white, he added. The UFO rose "vertically with the glow moving slowly around the perimeter in a clockwise direction, giving the appearance of a pinwheel."

Interpreter Ruben Efron told the CIA that visibility was excellent. As one UFO approached the train, he said, "the object gave the impression of gliding. No noise was heard and no exhaust was heard, and no exhaust glow or trail was seen by me." After the encounter, Senator Russell told the men with him: "We saw a flying disc. I wanted you boys to see it so that I would have witnesses," according to the CIA documents. And an FBI memo, dated November 4, 1955, also discusses the sighting-and admitted Col. Hathaway's testimony "would support existence of a flying disc" Dr. Maccabee, of the Fund for UFO Research, believes that Senator Russell and his group never publicly revealed their incredible sightings "because they were no doubt advised not to talk. These documents provide startling new evidence that UFO's exist."

Mr. Tom Towers, in his January 20, 1957, column, "Aviation News," for the Los Angeles, CA, Examiner, printed the contents of a letter from Senator Russell, which was in response to a request for information about the sightings in Russia. Mr. Towers had originally contacted Senator Russell's office by letter with the request that he be given permission to "break" the story. The Senator wrote: "Permit me to acknowledge your letters relative to reports that have come to you regarding aerial objects seen in Europe last year. I received your letter, but I have discussed this matter with the affected agencies of the government, and they are of the opinion that it is not wise to publicize this matter at this time. I regret very much that I am unable to be of assistance to you." The letter was dated January 17, 1956.

UFO Interest in Nuclear Tests

Full Report/Article

At about 7.46 P.M. (local time), on September 27, 1957, the Air Traffic Controller at Launceston airport, Tasmania, observed a strong white light to the east proceeding at DC3 speed towards Hobart. Met radar and Tower control at Hobart were alerted. At 8.23 P.M., the Met radar picked up a strong echo at 9 to 10 thousand feet heading towards Hobart. The trace was held for approximately 15 seconds, where upon the source appeared to accelerate with "a terrific burst of speed" and disappear.

Date September 27, 1957
Location Maralinga, South Australia

During September and October, 1957, nuclear weapons test series, code named ANTLER, were undertaken at Maralinga, South Australia, with kilotonne range nuclear explosions being detonated on September 25th and October 9th. The site was subject to intense security. During that period the integrity of the facility was challenged in an extraordinary fashion.

Just before dusk one evening Royal Air Force Corporal Derek Murray and some colleagues were called out of the Maralinga village canteen to witness a UFO hovering apparently silently over the airfield. The UFO was described as a "magnificent sight", being silver/blue in colour, of a metallic lustre, with a line of "windows" or "portholes" along its edge. Corporal Murray states that the object could be seen so clearly that they could make out what appeared to be plating on the objects surface.

The duty air traffic controller also ostensibly witnessed the spectacle. He allegedly checked Alice Springs and Edinburgh airfields who reported they did not have anything over their areas. No photographs were taken as the top security status of the area required that all cameras be locked away. These had to be signed in and out when used. After about 15 minutes (as dusk began to fall) the aerial object left swiftly and silently. In a statement to UK researcher Jenny Randles, which he also sent to me, Murray stated, "I swear to you as a practicing Christian this was no dream, no illusion, no fairy story - but a solid craft of metallic construction".

The Levelland, Texas Landings

Full Report/Article

One of the most baffling and most publicized cases of a close encounter of the second kind occurred in 1957 at Levelland, Texas. Actually, there were no less than eight well-documented reports of the same craft and seven more that were unverified; the seven called in by anonymous persons. Some of those who made their reports have kept their names secret. Sadly, this is the case in many UFO reports. Many of those who had thought they were doing the right thing have regretted their decisions later because of public ridicule. However, the Levelland case has many respectable witnesses who have come forward, especially several members of the Levelland Police Department who witnessed the fantastic sights of November, 2, 1957 in the town of about 10,000. To understand the full impact of this case, a chronological account is preferred.

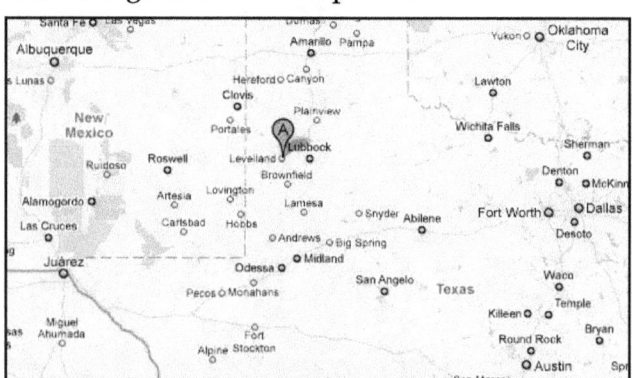

Date November 2, 1957
Location Levelland, Taxes, United States

11:00 P.M...Only one hour after the Russian Government launched their second dog-carrying satellite, and before America was aware of it, an unusual set of events began in the small town of Levelland. Patrolman A. J. Fowler was on desk duty when he received the first of fifteen different frantic phone calls in what would be an unforgettable night for him and his fellow officers. About four miles west of Levelland, Pedro Saucedo and his friend Joe Salaz were driving in Pedro's pickup truck when they saw a brightly lighted, cigar-shaped object moving in their direction. As the object approached, Pedro's car engine began to sputter, and his headlights went out. Finally, the car rolled to a stop. Later, a terrified Saucedo would sign a statement which indicated that the object was about 200 foot long. Calling Fowler from the small town of Whiteface, his call was dismissed by Fowler, who thought that the two men had been drinking.

11:45 P.M...Fowler receives a second call from a man identified only as Mr. W. The man was driving near the town of Whitharral, about four miles east of Levelland, when he came upon a brilliantly lit egg-shaped object, actually sitting on the pavement in the middle of the road. Mr. W's car engine stopped, and his headlights failed. Frightened, he left his vehicle, and after a brief period of time, the object silently lifted up to about 200 ft. and disappeared. His car started back up, and he sped away to make his phone call to Fowler.

12:00 A.M...Fowler receives a third call, this time from a man who was travelling 11 miles north of Levelland, when he spotted an unusual flying craft landed on the road. His car also faltered, and he sat watching the silent object for a brief period of time, until it rose up and disappeared into the night. Again, after the craft left the area, his car started, he left the scene, and called the Police station.

12:10 A.M... A nineteen year old freshman from Texas Tech University, Newell Wright, was driving 9 miles east of Levelland, when his car engine began to cut out, and his lights falter. After stopping his car and checking for some loose wire under the hood, he suddenly noticed a vivid object sitting on the pavement ahead of him. He described the object as about 125 foot long, and a bluish-green in colour. Frightened, he tried to start his car again to no avail. He sat in his car; hoping that another car would come by. None did.

After a little while, the object silently rose and faded away into the sky. Afraid to make a report, the young student waited to tell his parents when they arrived home from a trip. They encouraged him to report what he had seen. He made a statement at the Sheriff's office, and his report was included in the US Air Force's Project Blue Book.

12:15 A.M...Officer Fowler receives another call. This time from a man in a phone booth near Whitharral, who, as he was driving 9 miles north of Levelland, encountered an object of some kind sitting in the middle of the road. He had the same mechanical problems as the other motorists, and after the craft took off, his engine started again. At this point, Fowler's curiosity and concern motivated him to call the other patrol cars in the area, and report what he had heard from the different travellers. Later, he would state that "something odd" was going on. In a matter of a few minutes, two different Officers radioed in that they had seen two different flying objects with extremely bright lights, but had not yet encountered any engine problems.

12:45 A.M...A man driving west of Levelland very close to the spot of Saucedo's initial sighting, sees a large orange ball approaching in his direction. The man testifies that this unknown craft softly lands on the road about 1/4 mile away. The motorist also related a very interesting fact. He stated that the craft, orange at first, became a bluish-green colour upon landing on the road. He also noticed that the craft spanned the width of the road. After the craft landed, his engine also failed, and he sat in the cab of his truck, which was lit up by the glow from the craft. After a time, the craft lifted up and left the area. This man did not make a report at the time of the sighting, but did file a report the next day.

1:15 A.M... Fowler receives a call from a truck driver from Waco, Texas, who states that while driving northeast of Levelland, he witnessed a large, glowing object, and at the same time, his truck engine failed. Fowler noted that the caller was extremely frightened. The driver added that the object was about 200 ft. long, and after it left the area, his truck roared back to life, and he "got the hell out of there."

1:30 A.M...Fowler receives the first definite sighting of the object by two law enforcement officers. Sheriff Clem and Deputy

McCullough, who were receiving constant updates from Fowler, had observed a "large, glowing object," pass across the highway. The two officers were trying to track the object by the radio calls from Fowler. They were about 4-5 miles outside of Levelland when they saw the object. The two officers stated that the object looked like a large, red sun and it lit up the entire highway as it passed over.

The events of the night finally came to an end. Fowler would later state that he had received no less than fifteen calls from observers who claimed to have seen the unusual craft. He also said that they were legitimately excited, and some of them extremely frightened. The unusual number of witnesses to the Levelland events only solidified the theory that some unusual craft had been in the area of the city for at least 2 1/2 hours that night. The dramatic accounts of the landings on the road set this case off as one of the most convincing cases of an encounter with the unknown. The next day the small town of Levelland, Texas was bulging over with reporters, anxiously awaiting some official explanation for the events of the night before. The Air Force did investigate these sightings, but offered no reasonable cause for what was seen that night. The case is still considered "unexplained."

Frightened Dog Case

Full Report/Article

November 10, 1957. Mrs. Leita Kuhn had been going back and forth between her house and backyard dog kennels checking on an overheating stove on a snowy, windy night. About 1:20 A.M. everything was in order, so she shut the kennel door. The snow had stopped and it was dark, with no moon or stars visible.

Date November 10, 1957
Location Madison, Ohio, United States

As she stepped away from the kennel she saw a huge glowing object in back, about 60 feet above the ground. It was about 40 feet wide and 10 feet thick with a dome on top, and glowing with a phosphorescent light. The top was brilliant and it hurt her eyes to look at it. Puffs of apparent exhaust appeared around the bottom increasingly, until she became unnerved by the spectacle and ran in the house. When she looked out the window, the object apparently had disappeared. The time was 1:55 A.M.

She stayed up all night caring for an apparently frightened dog that subsequently died of cancer. A few days later she sought medical treatment for eye irritation and skin rash, and was advised to report it to Civil Defence because of suspected radiation effects. She developed an abnormal craving for honey, other sweets, and water. For nearly two years she experienced a variety of physical ailments, some painful and emotionally disturbing.

An Astronaut Speaks Out

Full Report/Article

Gordon Cooper was one of America's original astronauts. He helped pioneer this country's space exploration efforts when, aboard a tiny space capsule known as Mercury [Faith] 7, Cooper orbited the Earth for 34 hours, proving that man could live outside our atmosphere for prolonged periods.

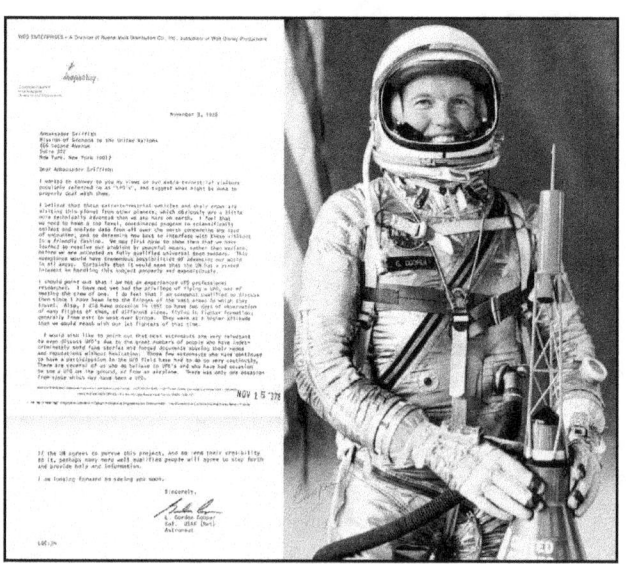

Date 1957 or 1958
Location Edwards AFB, United States

In the early 1950s, Cooper was assigned to a jet fighter group in Germany. While stationed there, he remembers very vividly the week an entire formation of circular objects passed over the Air Base on almost a daily routine.

'We never could get close enough to pin them down, but they were round in shape and very metallic looking,' Cooper points out. UFOs were to continue to haunt him when the Air Force Colonel was transferred several years later to Edwards Air Force Base Flight Test Centre in the California desert.

What happened one afternoon while he was on duty at this military base is evidence enough that the government definitely does keep a lot of secrets when it comes to UFOs!

The incident took place in the late 1950s, either 1957 or 1958 - as Cooper can best recall; and to this day, the photographic evidence of an actual UFO touching down upon the Earth is being kept under wraps.

During this period, Cooper was a Project Manager at Edwards Air Force Base, just three or four years before entering America's space programmeme. After lunch this particular day, Cooper had assigned a team of photographers to an area of the vast dry lake beds near Edwards.

In a taped interview with UFOlogist Lee Spiegel, the former Astronaut disclosed that while the crew was out there, they spotted a strange-looking craft above the lake bed, and they began taking films of it.

Cooper says the object was very definitely 'hovering above the ground. And then it slowly came down and sat on the lake bed for a few minutes.' All during this time the motion picture cameras were filming away.

'There were varied estimates by the cameramen on what the actual size of the object was,' Cooper confesses, 'but they all agreed that it was at least the size of a vehicle that would carry normal-sized people in it.'

Col. Cooper was not fortunate enough to be outside at the time of this incredible encounter, but he did see the films as soon as they were rushed through the development process.

'It was a typical circular-shaped UFO,' he recollects. 'Not too many people saw it, because it took off at quite a sharp angle and just climbed straight on out of sight!'

Cooper admits he didn't take any kind of poll to determine who had seen the craft, 'because there were always strange things flying around in the air over Edwards.' This is a statement Lee Spiegel was able to verify through his own research efforts, having obtained closely guarded tapes of conversations between military pilots circling the base and their commanding officers in the flight tower, tracking the presence of unknown objects.

'People just didn't ask a lot of questions about things they saw and couldn't understand,' notes Cooper, who adds that it was a lot simpler to look the other way, shrug one's shoulders, and chalk up what had been seen to 'just another experimental aircraft that must have been developed at another area of the air base.'

But what about the photographic proof - the motion picture footage - that was taken? 'I think it was definitely a UFO,' Cooper states, as he makes no bones about it. 'However, where it (the object) came from and who was in it is hard to determine, because it didn't stay around long enough to discuss the matter - there wasn't even time to send out a welcoming committee!'

After he reviewed the film at least a dozen times, the footage was quickly forwarded to Washington. Cooper no doubt expected to get a reply in a few weeks' time as to what his men had seen and photographed, but there was no word, and the movie *vanished* - never to surface again....

On coast-to-coast television, Cooper recently made a blockbuster statement that had the telephone lines tied up the next day, as viewers telephoned the stations which carried the syndicated Merv Griffin Show, anxious to find out if their ears had been playing tricks on them the night before.

Toward the end of the talk-show host's interview with the former Astronaut, Merv broke into a secretive tone of voice right on the air, and aimed a hundred-thousand-dollar question at his guest: 'There is a story going around, Gordon, that a spaceship did land in middle America and there were occupants, and members of our government were able to keep one of the occupants alive for a period of time. They've seen the metal of the aircraft and they know what the people look like - is that a credible story?'

For all intents and purposes Cooper should have laughed for assuredly such a speculative story belongs in the category of science fiction or space fantasy. But Gordon Cooper kept a straight face when he replied: 'I think it's fairly credible. I would like to see the time when all qualified people could really work together to properly investigate these stories and either refute or prove them.'

The bombshell had been dropped. Cooper went on to say that from the various reports of UFO contacts and abductions he had been privy to, he was convinced that the occupants of this crashed UFO were 'probably not that different from what we are,' - that they are almost totally humanoid (i.e., have two arms, two legs, a torso and readily identifiable facial features) in appearance.

Taken aback by what Cooper had said over the national airwaves, Lee Spiegel telephoned Cooper's office the following morning and managed to get past his private secretary, though others in the media were getting the cold shoulder.

'Cooper admitted to me that he could have revealed more on the air, but he decided not to play his entire hand because he felt certain that some 'official eyebrows were going to get raised'.'"

The Warminster Thing

Full Report / Article

In the mid-1960s a sleepy Wiltshire town became the unlikely epicentre of a UFO phenomenon.

Warminster, in West Wiltshire, became known globally for what was enigmatically called "The Thing". The Thing took many forms by those who claimed to have observed it between 1965 and 1977.

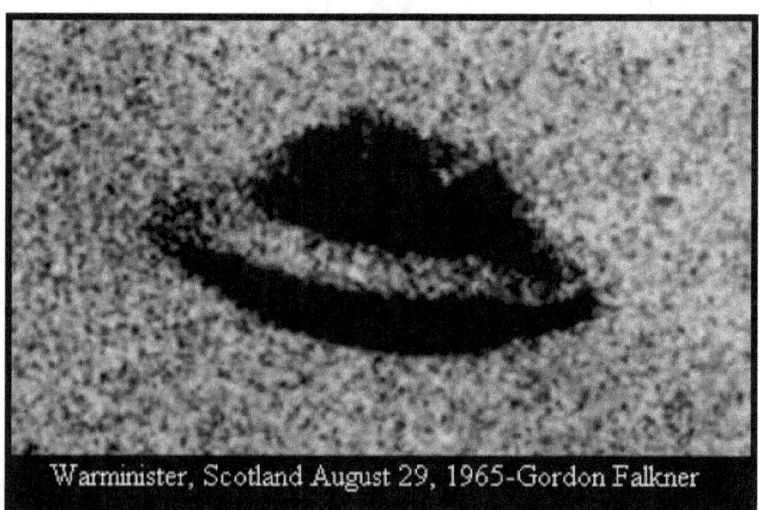
Warminster, Scotland August 29, 1965-Gordon Falkner

Date December, 1964
Location Warminster, West Wiltshire, United Kingdom

The first sign of The Thing was during the Christmas of 1964, when residents heard a loud, unidentifiable whine. The strange sightings were reported in the Warminster Journal. Local journalist Arthur Shuttlewood was instrumental in making the phenomenon national news and in one year more than 1000 sightings of unidentified flying objects were recorded.

They continued to be seen on a regular basis between 1965 and 1977, and in many ways formed a key chapter of the 1960s . Although there have been few sightings in recent years, Warminster is still seen by many as synonymous with UFOs.

With the army based on nearby Salisbury Plain, Warminster is well known as a military town. This gave rise to the theory that visitors from outer space could very well have been mistaken military aircraft.

But believers shrugged off this theory believing that the military were one of the reasons Warminster had been chosen for visitations. Whatever the reason for the coming of The Thing, it has certainly put Warminster on the map.

Florida Everglades Encounter

Full Report / Article

On March 12, 1965, James Flynn of East Fort Myers, Florida, an experienced woodsman, headed deep into the Everglades with his four hunting dogs. He had planned to spend several days there. On the night of the 14th his hunting dogs took after a deer. Later, hearing a sound like a gunshot, Flynn started up his swamp buggy and headed off in search of his dogs. One of his dogs had returned, which he had placed in its cage, and it accompanied him on his search for the others.

Date March 15, 1965
Location Everglades, Florida, United States

Around 1 A.M., on Monday, March 15th, Flynn spotted something unusual that he judged to be slightly over a mile away. Whatever it was, it was hovering, shaped like a broad, upside-down cone, an estimated 200 feet in the air above some cypress trees. After a while it began flying off toward the Northeast. After some 2 to 3 minutes, it returned to the same place, and hovered again, this time for an estimated 5 minutes. Then it took off toward the Southwest at a high rate of speed. Soon, however, it returned to the same location again. At this point, Flynn was only about a quarter of a mile away, and the object seemed to come down among some trees into a small knoll. Flynn figured, up to this point, that he was observing a helicopter of some sort, but then he began to study it through a pair of binoculars and he realized that he wasn't looking at a helicopter at all. Then he began to suspect that it was some secret craft from Cape Canaveral.

Flynn described the object as some 25 feet high, and twice that in its diameter. Up near the top were four tiers of two-foot-square square window-looking sections that emitted a yellowish glow. The thing was metallic, and seemed to be made of four-by-four plates that appeared to be held together with rivets. Around the base there was an orange-red illumination that seemed to cast a glow on the ground some 75 feet around its rim.

Sometime later he regains consciousness. Finding himself initially blind he lays there for a long while until he recovers a small amount of vision in his left eye. By this time, the sun is shining and its Tuesday morning. Flynn gathers up his dogs and makes his way to the home of Henry Osceola, a Seminole Indian who lived there in the Everglades swamp.

It isn't until noon Wednesday that Flynn returns home. He and his wife go immediately to pay a visit to ophthalmologist, Paul R. Brown. Dr. Brown finds Flynn's vision 20/800 in his right eye, 20/60 in his left eye. He notes a slight bruise over his right brow. The left eye appeared normal, but in the right eye he could not see the retina.

Flynn complained of hearing reduction and numbness in his arms and hands following the encounter. Under careful observation and treatment by Dr. Harvie J. Stipe, a physician who had known Flynn for 25 years, Flynn was treated, and soon those symptoms disappeared. On March 26, Flynn, Dr. Stipe, and two others, returned to the encounter site in the Everglades, and there found a burned circle some 72 feet across. The circle looked like it had been swept clean of leaves, twigs, limbs -- normal forest debris. Eight cypress trees were scorched from their tops down to about halfway from the ground.

In October 1966, in a phone interview with Arizona physicist James E. McDonald, Flynn stated that the UFO was probably, he figured, some secret aircraft, and that if he could ever prove it then somebody would pay for the good eye he used to have.

In July 1996, Flynn made a rare public appearance at Port Charlotte, Florida, where he stated: "I'm waiting for the day someone turns up the truth about this thing. I hope I live that long."

The Tully Saucer Nest

Full Report/Article

At 9:00 A.M. on January 19, 1966, a calm sunny day, a 28 year old banana farmer named George Pedley was driving a tractor near Horseshoe Lagoon on the property of Albert Pennisi, near Tully, in tropical far north Queensland, Australia. When he was about 25 yards from the lagoon, he heard a loud hissing sound above the noise of the tractor.

Date January 19, 1966
Location Tully, Queensland, Australia

Suddenly, an object rose out of the swamp. When I glanced at it, it was already 30 feet above the ground, and at about tree-top level.

It was a large, grey, saucer-shaped object, convex on the top and bottom and measured some 25 feet across and 9 feet high. While I watched, it rose another 30 feet, spinning very fast, then it made a shallow dive and took off with tremendous speed. Climbing at an angle of 45 degrees it disappeared within seconds in a south-westerly direction...

Another surprise came when Pedley rounded the bend of the road and came to the spot from which the object had risen. There in the lagoon was a large circular area that was clear of reeds and in which the water was rotating slowly. It had not been like that three hours earlier when he had passed the lagoon. After looking around, he got back on the tractor and left.

A few hours later, at about noon, Pedley returned to the lagoon for a second look. The scene had changed, because now the circular area was covered by a floating mass of green reeds that were distributed in a clockwise radial pattern. The circular mass of reeds was about 30 feet in diameter.

Pedley was by now excited enough about what he was seeing to go and tell Albert Pennisi, the owner of the sugar cane farm land on which the lagoon was located, and another friend. Pennesi recalled that his dog had acted strangely that morning, barking madly and heading off toward the lagoon at about 5:30 A.M. Pennisi and the other man were amazed by the circular mass of reeds. Wading out to the mass, they found that they could swim under the mass of reeds and that the lagoon floor beneath it was smooth and showed no traces of roots. Oddly, the outside edges of the mass of reeds angled down, similar to the shape of a saucer placed face down. Pennisi went and got his camera and took photographs of the mass of reeds, which was now beginning to turn brown on its top surface. George Pedley reported his experience to the Tully police that evening, and they in turn reported it to the RAAF after making a trip to the site the next day, January 20th.

Within days, the media had picked up the event and the area was filled with investigators, many of whom were trying to prove theories as to the cause of the "nest" such as helicopters, big birds, crocodiles, reed-eating grubs, and whirlwinds of one sort or another. Pedley's UFO sighting was all but overlooked in the flurry of explanations. During the course of the investigations, as many as five other "nests", all smaller than the original, were discovered. In some of these, the reeds were rotated in a counter-clockwise direction and a couple of them showed signs of burning in the centre of the nest. Samples of the original nest were sent to Brisbane for analysis, but nothing unusual was detected. Other than being part of the "nest", the only unusual thing about the reeds was that they turned brown in about 8 hours, whereas reeds uprooted by hand in the lagoon took three days to turn brown.

In another unusual twist, Albert Pennisi told a reporter from the Sydney, Australia newspaper The Sun that he had been dreaming about a UFO landing on his property for a week:

I'd get them almost every night. And they were beginning to worry me. I couldn't understand them. It was always the same. This thing like a giant dish would come out of nowhere and land nearby.

And I would watch it in my dream and get real afraid before it went away. Then on Wednesday morning about 5 o'clock my dog suddenly seemed to go out of its mind. It was howling like a mad thing and raced off towards the lagoon.

What happened at Horseshoe Lagoon? There was never any evidence that there were any helicopters in the area nor any demonstrated reason for one to be over the lagoon. There was no evidence that crocodiles made the nest and analysis of the reeds from the nest showed no trace of "reed-eating grubs." There was no known bird that would or could make such a nest in three hours.

The best explanation that the RAAF could offer was that the nest was created by a willy willy, a type of small whirlwind known to occur in the area.

Although a conclusive determination could not be made, the most probable explanation was that the sighting was of a "willy willy" or circular wind phenomenon which flattened the reeds and sucked up debris to a height of about 30 feet, thus forming what appeared to be a "flying saucer", before moving off and dissipating. Hissing noises are known to be associated with "willy willies" and the theory is also substantiated by the clockwise configuration of the depression.

However, such whirlwinds, except when they occur in the desert as dust devils, normally accompany thunderstorms, and although the Tully event occurred during the rainy season, January 19 was a sunny day with little or no wind. Pedley described what he saw as a blue-grey object shaped like two saucers face to face. This description doesn't sound like a whirling mass of swamp debris, and there was no fallen debris in the area where the dissipation would have occurred. Finally, how does the whirlwind explanation account for the fact that the water was clear when Pedley looked the first time, yet was covered by the mass of reeds when he looked again three hours later?

Bizarre UFO Encounter over Texas Uranium Mine

Full Report/Article
The summer of 1971, Marcus Harvey was working the night shift for Conoco Oil Co. at an open pit uranium mine west of Karnes City Texas.

Date Summer of 1971
Location Karnes City, Texas, United States

Harvey was one of 6 people operating Caterpillar 657B earth movers. We were down to about 210 feet deep when this incident happened. It was about 11:10 P.M., just after shift change they were getting ready to crank there machines, when the 85 acre pit lit up as if it was daylight. The light was so bright that he had to squint because it hurt his eyes. He remembers hearing a high pitched hissing noise and the hair on his arms stood on end. He was so scared, He fell to the ground and started praying.

He remembers trying to look up, but the light was so bright he couldn't. After about 2 minutes, the light started getting dimmer and he could finally look up at it. What he saw amazed him. The object was round and the bright light was coming from the centre of the bottom of the UFO. Around the perimeter of the craft was hundreds of penlight size light beams that alternated in all colours of the spectrum. Now he knows they were laser beams. The UFO was rising up slowly at first and then went straight up out of sight in about 10 seconds. He was crying and shaking and so was everyone else. The other shift workers thought they were crazy.

There is a vein of uranium ore that runs from George West Texas to almost Texarkana Texas. When determining where to place a mine, the following steps are accomplished: (1) A geologist with a geiger counter flies over the area and finds the highest radiation reading. (2) Drilling trucks are sent out and core samples are drilled to determine the highest concentration of uranium ore. These core samples are drilled in a grid pattern and every core sample is given a tracking number and logged in showing the concentration and amount of uranium present. (3) The open pit mine is then laid out according to these core samples.

When this UFO incident happened, they were about 2 feet away from a layer of hard rock called the "tap rock" that laid directly on top of the uranium ore. The uranium ore varied in depth from 6 to 18 inches and had about the same brown colour as low grade coal. Two days after this incident, the tap rock was removed to expose the uranium ore. They were astounded to find that the uranium ore was now a chalky white substance that had NO radioactivity at all! There was a 250 foot diameter circle of this chalky material in the centre of the pit.

Outside of the circle, the uranium ore was still as potent as before the incident. Core samples don't lie. This chalky material was uranium before this incident.

Soviet Cosmonaut sees Close-Up of UFO

Full Report/Article

"It followed us during half of our orbit. We observed it on the light side, and when we entered the shadow side, it disappeared completely. It was an engineered structure, made from some type of metal, approximately 40 meters long with inner hulls. The object was narrow here and wider here, and inside there were openings. Some places had projections like small wings. The object stayed very close to us. We photographed it, and our photos showed it to be 25 to 29 meters away." - Cosmonaut Victor Afanasyev commenting on a UFO sighting that occurred while en route to the Solyut 6 space station in April 1979.

Date April 1979
Location Space

Cosmonaut Adanasyev made a drawing of the space ship he witnessed from aboard the Soviet orbital vessel.

Victor states, "I think we are not alone, something of extraterrestrial origin has visited Earth." The alien craft turned toward ours, followed us and flew formation 25 to 29 meters away. We photographed the metallic engineering structure that was around 40 meters long. The film was later confiscated.

Hudson Valley Sightings

Full Report/Article

The Hudson Valley UFO account is composed of not one, but many sightings, all similar, and all pointing to one conclusion. There was something "unexplained" going on in this place only an hour's drive north of New York City. The Hudson Valley UFO saga began at almost the beginning of a new year, 1982. Just a short time before midnight, December 31, 1981, a retired policeman was sitting in his backyard in Kent, N. Y. He saw a group of strange lights to the south. The lights were a brilliant red, green, and white, and at first, he thought they could be coming from an airplane in trouble. It was common for him to sit and watch the big jets fly over at night. As the lights became closer, his opinion quickly changed. The lights were moving too slowly to be a plane, and now...they were too low, and there was no noise from an engine. What was the strange craft he was seeing?

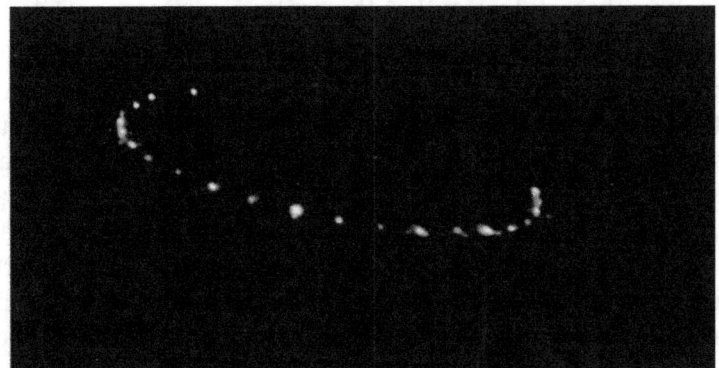

Date December 31, 1981
Location Hudson Valley, New York, United States

As the lights came closer, he could hear a humming sound, and now he could see that the lights were arranged in a triangular shape, and there was a solid object of some kind connecting the lights. No, this was no aircraft he had ever seen before! The solid part looked like ..like..a fuselage. That's what it was..a fuselage. He was looking at a UFO. This type of report would be repeated many times in the Hudson Valley over the next few years. All of them were similar, a V-shaped row of lights connected by a solid object of some type. Literally hundreds of witnesses would see this same sight. There was definitely something unusual going on in the skies over the Hudson Valley. Something that moved ever so slowly, so silently.

On March 26, 1983, an article about the sightings appeared on the front page of the Westchester-Rockland Daily Item. The article recounted the many reports of the strange phenomena. The cat was out of the bag. The press coverage drew the attention of a group of UFO investigators which was associated with Dr. J. Allen Hynek, acclaimed scientist and UFO investigator. A thorough investigation followed, and ultimately a book, "Night Siege: The Hudson Valley UFO Sightings," written by Dr. Hynek and Philip J. Imbrogno.

The group began their inquiries by setting up a phone hotline. They received over 300 calls from individuals who had seen the strange V-shaped lights on the night of March 24, 1983 alone. Descriptions were very similar, if not identical. The object always moved slowly, and almost silently. It always had many lights, and they were always in a V-configuration. Some of the witnesses got a close enough look to say that the craft was large enough to be a "flying city."

On the same night, the city of Yorktown also came alive with reports of this giant flying craft. The police switchboard was jammed with so many calls about the UFO that they feared not being able to respond to "real emergencies." Drivers pulled over on the Taconic parkway to watch the large object slowly make it's way across the skies. All in all, about 5,000 reports were made during a period of five years, from 1982 through 1986. The object was seen by multiple witnesses at night, but never was a report made of it appearing during daylight hours. The sightings ranged as far east as New Haven, Connecticut, and as far north as Brookfield, Connecticut.

Several theories were put forth about whether there was only one object, or many. Some additional accounts would come forward stating that the object, though moving slowly, would at times make a rapid, fast manoeuvre from one location to another. Also the lights of the craft could change colours in an instant.

A report made from guards at the Indian Point Nuclear Plant would be one of the most dramatic. The gigantic UFO was seen hovering over the plant for periods of time, and moved as close as 30 feet from the reactor. Security supervisors even once considered ordering in planes to have it show down. The object over Indian Point was described by some of the guards as 1,000 ft. long. Another witness described the object hovering over the Croton Falls Reservoir, using a red beam as it seemed to scan the surface of the water. Reasonable explanations for the sightings were offered. Skeptics suggested that planes, balloons, satellites, the planet Venus, etc, could explain away the accounts. Considering all of the information available, researchers could find only one object that could mimic the movements of the UFO, a blimp. All blimp manufacturers and pilots were contacted, and not one case of a blimp over the area on the nights of the sightings could be found. The Hudson Valley sightings are still a mystery to this day.

Japanese Airline 1628 Encounters UFO

Full Report / Article

It was just a routine flight. Well, not exactly routine.... It was a special Japan Air Lines 747 cargo flight to carry a load of French wine from Paris to Tokyo. The flight plan would carry flight 1628 from Paris to Reykjavik, Iceland, across the North Atlantic and Greenland, then across Canada to Anchorage, Alaska, and finally across the Pacific to Tokyo. The crew consisted of veteran Captain Kenju Terauchi, co-pilot Takanori Tamefuji, and flight engineer Yoshio Tsukuba. On November 16, 1986, laden with wine, JAL1628 took off from Paris and flew the first leg of the trip, to Reykjavik. The next day, they continued, flying over Greenland and then across northern Canada without event.

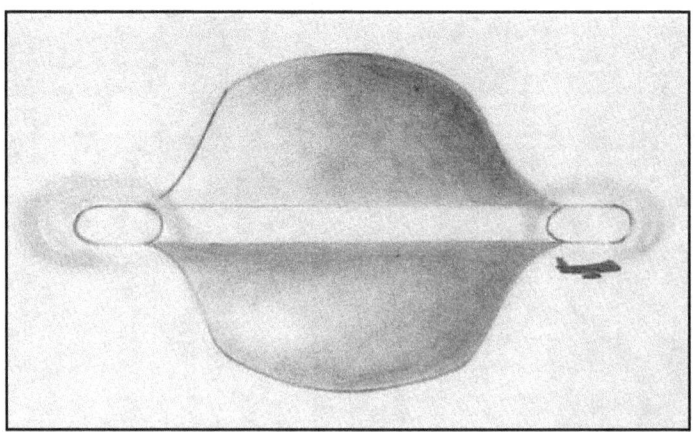

Date November 17, 1986
Location Northeastern Alaska, United States

Just after they crossed into Alaska, at 5:09 P.M. local time, Anchorage Air Traffic Control contacted them on the radio to report initial radar contact. The Anchorage flight controller asked them to turn 15 degrees to the left and head for a point known as Talkeetna on a heading of 215 degrees. They were at 35,000 feet and traveling at a ground speed of about 600 mph. At about 5:11 P.M. local time, Captain Terauchi noticed the lights of some sort of aircraft about 2000 feet below and 30 degrees to the left front of them. He decided that the aircraft was probably an American jet fighter from nearby Eielson or Elmendorf Air Force Bases patrolling Alaskan airspace, so he ignored them at first. However, after a few minutes, he noticed that the lights were keeping pace with his own aircraft, which would be an unusual thing for patrolling jets to do.

"It was about seven or so minutes since we began paying attention to the lights (when), most unexpectedly, two spaceships stopped in front of our face, shooting off lights. The inside cockpit shined brightly and I felt warm in the face." Terauchi said that it was his impression that the two objects he had seen below them minutes before had suddenly jumped in from of him. The craft, one above the other, kept pace with the 747 for several minutes, moving in unison with an odd rocking motion. After about seven minutes, they changed to a side-by-side arrangement. Terauchi said that the "amber and whitish" lights were like flames coming out of multiple rocket exhaust ports arranged in two rectangular rows on the craft. He felt that they fired in a particular sequence to stabilize the craft, much like the small manoeuving thrusters on the Space Shuttle. He also reported seeing sparks like a fire when using gasoline or carbon fuel.

Co-pilot Tamefuji described the lights as "Christmas assorted" lights with a "salmon" colour. He said: I remember red or orange, and white landing light, just like a landing light. And weak green, ah, blinking. He also described the lights as pulsating slowly. They became stronger, became weaker., became stronger, became weaker, different from strobe lights. The lights were "swinging" in unison as if there were "very good formation flight...close" of two aircraft side by side. He described the appearance of the lights as similar to seeing "night flight head-on traffic", where it is only possible to see the lights on an approaching aircraft and "we can not see the total shape." He said, "I'm sure I saw something. It was clear enough to make me believe that there was an oncoming aircraft." Flight engineer Tsukuba, who sat behind the copilot, did not have as good a view of the lights. He first saw them "through the L1 window at the 11 o'clock position" and he saw "clusters of lights undulating". These clusters were "made of two parts...shaped like windows of an airplane". He emphasized that "the lights in front of us were different from town lights." He described the colours as white or amber.

Tamefuji decided to call Anchorage Air Traffic Control, and for the next thirty minutes the 747 and AARTCC were in constant contact regarding the UFO. During this time, Captain Terauchi asked Tskububa to hand him a camera so that he could attempt to take a photograph of the lights. However, Terauchi was unfamiliar with the camera and could not get it to operate. Tsukuba also could not get his camera to operate due to problems with the auto-focus and finally gave up trying to take a photo. At this point they began experiencing some radio interference and were asked by Anchorage to change frequencies. Terauchi later said that Anchorage kept asking him about clouds in the immediate area: They asked us several times if there were clouds near our altitude. We saw thin and spotty clouds near the mountain below us, no clouds in mid-to-upper air, and the air current was steady.

Soon after the exchanges about clouds, the objects flew off to the left. Terauchi said later: "There was a pale white flat light in the direction where the ships flew away, moving in a line along with us, in the same direction and same speed and at the same altitude as we were."

Terauchi decided to see whether they could see anything on the 747's own radar:

"I thought it would be impossible to find anything on an aircraft radar if a large ground radar did not show anything, but I judged the distance of the object visually and it was not very far. I set the digital weather radar distance to 20 (nautical) miles, radar angle to horizon (i.e., no depression angle). There it was on the screen. A large green and round object had appeared at 7 or 8 miles (13 km to 15 km) away, where the direction of the object was. We reported to Anchorage centre that our radar caught the object within 7 or 8 miles in the 10 o'clock position. We asked them if they could catch it on ground radar but it did not seem they could catch it at all " At 5:25:45, after spending two minutes looking, the military radar at Elmendorf Regional Operational Control Centre also picked up something. The ROCC radar controller reported back to the AARTCC that he was getting some "surge primary return." By this he meant an occasional radar echo unaccompanied by a transponder signal.

As the 747 neared Fairbanks:

"The lights (of the city) were extremely bright to eyes that were used to the dark. (The cockpit lights had been turned off to eliminate window reflections of internal lights.) We were just above the bright city lights and we checked the pale white light behind us. Alas! There was a silhouette of a gigantic spaceship. We must run away quickly! "Anchorage Centre. The JAL1628 is requesting a change of course to right 45 degrees." It felt like a long time before we received permission just after the plane turned to the right, the AARTCC controller called the Fairbanks Approach Radar controller to find out whether or not the short-range radar had a target near the JAL. The approach radar reported no target other than JAL1628. "

The plane came out of the turn and flew toward Talkeetna at an altitude of 31,000 ft, with the object still following. At about 5:40 a United Airlines passenger jet took off from Anchorage and headed north to Fairbanks. The AARTCC controller decided to ask the UA pilot to try to see the object that was following the JAL flight. The UA pilot said he would look when he got closer. The controller asked the JAL flight to stay at 31,000 ft and the UA flight to stay at 29,000 ft. He then directed the UA flight to turn some more so that the planes would pass within five miles of one another.

As the United Airlines jet got closer, the UFO apparently dropped behind, allowing the JAL plane to get far ahead. The United pilot asked the AARTCC to have the JAL pilot flash the headlights on the JAL aircraft so he could locate the plane. At 5:49:45 the JAL pilot did that. At this point the planes were about 25 miles apart. When the planes were about 12 miles apart, the UA plane reported seeing the JAL plane and nothing else. But by this time the UFO had apparently disappeared, not being seen by JAL1628, either.

At about 5:51, the AARTCC requested that a military TOTEM

flight in the area also fly toward the JAL plane for a look. During the next several minutes TOTEM viewed the JAL plane but couldn't see any other traffic. JAL1628 proceeded to Anchorage and landed at 6:20 P.M. The FAA conducted an investigation of the incident, and did not issue its final report until March 5. CSICOP's (Committee for the Scientific Investigation of Claims of the Paranormal) Phil Klass issued a premature statement on January 22 claiming that the UFOs were the planets Jupiter and Mars - an impossible solution because the UFO was seen in a part of the sky opposite the position of these planets and because the UFOs moved from positions one above the other to side by side. CSICOP later issued a second explanation that the UFO was light reflecting off of clouds of ice crystals - also unlikely because the sky was clear at the reported altitude of the UFO. The FAA attributed the radar images received by ground radar to a "split radar return from the JAL Boeing 747."

Florida Police Patrolman Encounters UFO

Full Report/Article

Just before 4 A.M. on March 19, 1992, Patrolman Luis Delgado, 28, of the Haines City, Fla., Police Department frantically radioed his dispatcher. He said that a light had begun following him after he steered his cruiser down a dark street alongside a citrus grove. He requested assistance.

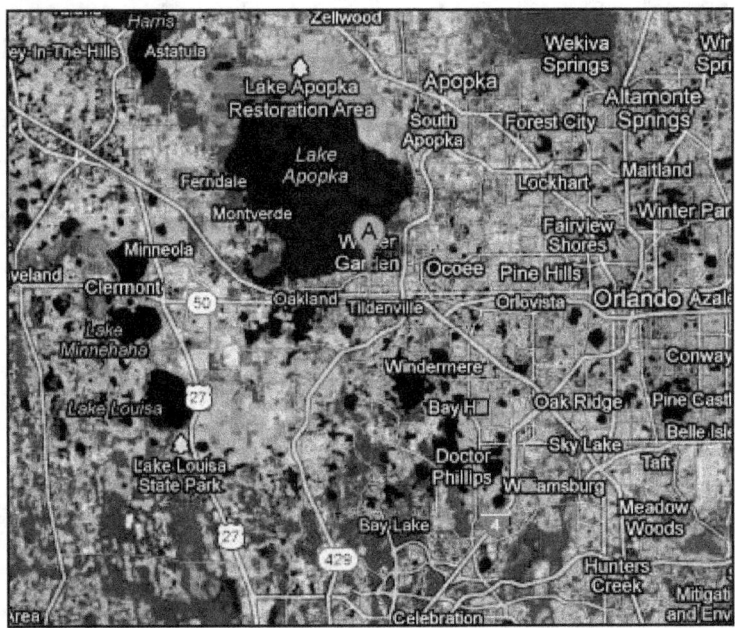

Date March 19, 1992
Location Haines City, Florida, United States

His story, which he would tell fellow officers, is a strange one. Delgado said he noticed a rapidly-descending bright green light in his rearview mirror, and that, seconds later the interior of the car lit up as the light moved to his right and began to pace the car at about 40 miles per hour. When he slowed his patrol car, the light manoeuvreed in front of him. Though it was so brilliant he had to squint, what he saw behind the glow shocked him. It appeared to be a metallic dome-shaped object, about 15 feet wide, hovering over the road.

Delgado pulled his car over to a stop and as he did its engine, lights, and police radio all died. The object continued to hover soundlessly about 10 feet off the pavement and 20 feet in front of his vehicle. Delgado got out of his car and began stepping backward down the street, feeling panic. He noticed that his breath fogged as if it were a cold morning, yet the temperature was 60 degrees. The object departed silently, and Delgado returned to his patrol car where, he says, the ignition, lights, and police radio all started up again without his assistance.

At 3:56 A.M., four minutes after Delgado made his distress call, three patrol cars roared up. Sergeant H.L. Bartley found Delgado sitting in his cruiser with the door open, shaking.

Later that morning Delgado underwent both a physical and a psychological examination, neither of which found any evidence of injury or mental abnormality. Sgt. Bartley, now retired from the force, vouches for Delgado's credibility. "I don't doubt he saw something strange out there that morning."

More than seven years after the incident Delgado, who has not spoken to the media until now, thinks every day about what happened to him. "It's still so vivid in my mind. It was the strangest experience of my life."

Mark Rodeghier, Ph.D., scientific director of the Centre for UFO Studies in Chicago, calls Delgado's experience similar to nearly 500 others he has cataloged. "The Delgado encounter fits a pattern we have observed since 1947 of UFOs, whatever they are, adversely affecting engines and electrical systems."

St. Petersburg, Russia Incident

Full Report/Article

The St. Petersburg incident is one of the most witnessed and highly recorded incidents in the history of Ufology. The events took place in the skies over St. Petersburg in Russia on the evening of February 19, 1997, when at around 7:00 P.M. The residents of the city became aware of a cluster of lights hovering overhead. The incident was unusual in that there were multiple witnesses; a number of video recordings made and was seen quite clearly by air traffic staff and aircrew at the local airport. Just after 7:00 P.M. the air traffic controllers at the local airport saw the strange objects appear on their radar screens and also strange lights became quite visible in the skies over the airport. One of the air traffic controllers, Victor Laxtushin, went outside and witnessed the objects, he remarked:

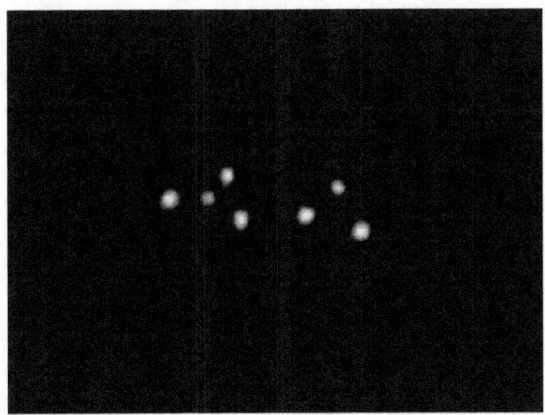

Date February 19, 1997
Location St. Petersburg, Russia

"I sketched the event as it happened; the shape of the lights changed, left and then re-appeared. Others were watching through binoculars. There was an aircraft on the runway - they confirmed the presence of a UFO. I am perhaps better qualified than most witnesses but I can't say what it was - experimental craft? But why fly experimental aircraft over St. Petersburg?" By 7:15 P.M. the strange lights had now apparently formed into a "triangle" and reports of the UFO were coming in from many different locations and many people captured the incident on video tape. He remains perplexed by the whole event.

Uri Arzamastsev, an economics student, noticed the lights, high in the sky and well above the horizon, through the kitchen window - rushing outside with his camcorder he captured the UFO on video and, by this time, the rest of his family were also witnessing the event.

The incident was later officially investigated by Naval Captain Pavel Syrchenko, who after collecting all the evidence was unable to explain the event away as military or civilian aircraft, balloons etc.

The objects hovered over the city for about 20 minutes and at 7:20 P.M. they could not be seen. There are many similarities between the St. Petersburg incident and the series of events which became known as "The Phoenix Lights". In both cases the appearance of a "triangular-shaped" craft was heralded by strange lights in the sky.

Alien Encounters

On September 9, 2005, villagers in Thailand claimed they witnessed an "alien" or extra-terrestrial being which appeared like a small-body man with large head and about 70 centimeters tall. Over 10 residents of Huay Rak Village in Mae Jan district's Tombom Janjawa said they saw the ET today morning in a rice field outside the village.

Like many people, perhaps you think of extra-terrestrials as merely the stuff of science fiction movies and hardly to be taken seriously. If this indeed the case as far as you are concerned, than you are in for quite a surprise. For within the pages of this fascinating book, you will find numerous accounts of close encounters that at first seem beyond belief, and yet are within the experiences of scores of serious, reliable witnesses from all over the world.

Aliens, as you are about to discover from such reports, seem to visit 20-century Planet Earth on a fairly regular basis. Not only that, they also occasionally abduct human beings for their own purposes.

Extra-terresrials come in many shapes and sizes, according to those who have met with them. Some also seem to pose something of considerable threat.

But are such encounters necessarily part of an objective reality? Would you see aliens, too, if present at the time of a supposed visitation? Or maybe these are really just 'encounters of the mind' and thus purely subjective experiences, taking place for one individual only?

Psychologists have also long been fascinated by the possibility that today's extra-terrestrials are simply the modern equivalent angels, fairies or demons. Or could it perhaps be the other way around? Were early accounts of winged chariots and fantastic beasts actually alien sightings?

We invite you to decide for yourself as you join us in a broad investigation of the entire alien encounter phenomenon.

Voronezh, Russia UFO Landing and Aliens

Full Report/Article

One of the most bizarre accounts of UFO folklore involves an incident that allegedly occurred in Voronezh, Russia. This case was reported in the United States by the St. Louis dispatch. The story was originally published on October 11, 1989, in America, but its origin was the Russian newspaper TASS.

Date September 27, 1989
Location Voronezh, Russian Federation

The report recounts the adventures of several young children who claimed to have seen a three-eyed alien with a robot escort.

The alien was said to be about nine foot tall. The craft, according to eye witness testimony, landed on the outskirts of the city. Shortly thereafter, the tall alien appeared, and upon seeing the young lad, shot a type of weapon at him, causing him to vanish before the eyes of the other people around him.

There are several important elements one must keep in mind regarding this extremely strange case of a close encounter. The original details of the case were brought forward by Genrikh Silanov, head of the Voronezh Geophysical Laboratory, who gave details to the TASS agency. Silanov stated that the media took an enormous amount of creative freedom with his report.

"Don't believe all you hear from Tass," he stated." We never gave them part of what they published."

I take this statement to mean that only a part of the news agency's report was based on the facts obtained from Silanov.

The agency had informed the entire world that Russian scientists had confirmed that an alien spaceship carrying giants with tiny heads had landed in Voronezh, a city of over 800,000 people located about 300 miles southeast of Moscow. They stated that as many as three of these giant creatures had emerged from the alien ship. The ship was described as a large, shining ball. These strange creatures were said to have walked in a nearby park, accompanied by a menacing robot. Ironically, TASS was the only media member to print the story in Russia. The newspaper Pravda declined to print, or comment on the strange tale.

In defence of the TASS account, Soviet reporter Skaya Kultura said that the agency was following the "the golden rule of journalism." "The reader must know everything."

The TASS account stated that the UFO landed in Voronezh on September 27, 1989, at 6:30 P.M. Young boys playing soccer witnessed the event, stating that a pinkish glow preceded the descent of the unusual flying craft. The pink glow became a deep red as it touched down. Most witnesses described the object as a flattened, disc shape. A crowd quickly gathered, and peered through a hatch that opened. They saw a "three-eyed alien" about 10 feet tall, clad in silvery overalls and bronze-coloured boots and wearing a disk on his chest. "

The TASS account also stated: "A boy screamed with fear, but when the alien gazed at him, with eyes shining, he fell silent, unable to move. Onlookers screamed, and the UFO and the creatures disappeared."

According to the report, about five minutes later, they reappeared. The alien had an object similar to a pistol - a tube about 20 inches long, which it pointed at an unidentified 16-year-old boy, making him disappear. The alien went inside the sphere, which then took off. At the same time, the boy reappeared.

"Children and eyewitnesses of the abnormal phenomenon have been questioned by police workers and journalists," wrote E. Efremov, the Voronezh correspondent for Soviet Skaya Kultura."

"There are no discrepancies in the description of the sphere itself or the actions of the aliens. Moreover, all the children who became witnesses to this event are still afraid, even now."

TASS listed three witnesses' names, all of whom were youngsters. They also stated that a group of international researchers would be investigating the claims of the witnesses.

Voronezh residents interviewed later claimed they had observed this UFO not just during the above incident but also many times on September 21, 23, 29 and October 2, between 6 and 9 P.M. Some of these incidents involved a different entity: small, with grayish-green face and blue overcoat resembling a loose raincoat.

This phenomenal account is still in need of more eye witness testimony and research. The Voronezh landing remains an unsolved mystery.

The Alfred Burtoo Encounter

Full Report/Article
Night Fishing

As 77-year-old Alfred Burtoo was fishing the Basingstoke Canal in the peaceful early hours of the morning of August 12, 1983, he saw a brilliant light descend from the sky and settle on the nearby towpath. Thinking it must be a helicopter from the nearby MOD base, he took no notice, and poured himself a cup of tea from his Thermos flask. Then his dog, Tiny, began whining furiously and two figures emerged from the darkness.

Date August 12, 1983
Location Aldershot, Hampshire, United Kingdom

"They were about four foot high, dressed in pale green coveralls from head to foot," Burtoo told reporters. "And they had helmets of the same colour with a visor that was blacked out."

The strangers gestured to Burtoo to accompany them. Calmly setting down his cup of tea, the intrepid pensioner followed them along the towpath towards a saucer-shaped craft. "I was 77 and didn't have much to lose," he later explained.

Inside the Saucer

Climbing up a set of steps into the saucer, Burtoo discovered that the ceiling was so low he had to stoop. He found himself inside a black, metallic octagonal chamber, which smelt slightly of decaying meat.

"I did not see any signs of nuts or bolts, nor did I see any seams where the object had been put together," he recalled. "What did interest me most of all was a shaft that rose up from the floor to the ceiling. The shaft was about four feet in circumference, and on the right-hand side stood two forms similar to those that walked along the towpath with me." One of the beings told the old man to stand beneath an orange light, which appeared to scan him for a few minutes. "What is your age?" asked the entity, in a "sing-song" voice which sounded like "a mixture of Chinese and Russian". When he replied that he was 78, it declared: "You can go. You are too old and infirm for our purposes." Bemused, Burtoo climbed down from the saucer and returned to his fishing spot.

"The first thing I did...was to pick up my cold cup of tea and drink it," he recalled. "And then I heard this whining noise, just as if an electric generator was starting up, and this thing lifted up then took off at a very high speed."

Apparently unfazed by his bizarre encounter, Burtoo resumed the task at hand. "I got into what I had come out for - the fishing!" Despite his rather curt reception, he later declared his nocturnal adventure to have been "the greatest experience of my life".

Quality Control?

Alfred Burtoo is not alone in having apparently failed an alien medical test. American abductee Carl Higdon believed that he had been rejected as a guinea pig for a hybrid breeding programme because his captors discovered that he had had a vasectomy. Likewise, Luis Oswald, an elderly Brazilian abducted in 1979 by beings who claimed to be from "a small galaxy near Neptune", reported that she had endured a lengthy examination then been told she was "of no use".

Forester Encounters Mine-like Entities in Scotland (the Dechmont Woods Encounter)

Full Report / Article
THE SCOTTISH LANDING CASE

The February 1980 (Vol. 28, #8) issue of the Bulletin contained a preliminary report on the alleged encounter of a West Lothian, Scotland forester with a strange object and equally strange smaller objects or "entities". The "happening" took place on November 9, 1979, and the following is the information gleaned from additional clippings and mainly from the Journal of Transient Aerial Phenomena, Vol.1, No.2, March, 1980. Strangely enough, the article was written by Stuart Campbell, the architect who initially identified

Date November 9, 1979
Location Livingston, Scotland, United Kingdom

the object(s) as manifestation(s) of ball lightning. However, it does seem that Mr. Campbell is being fairly objective, and the following are the "gleanings". We refer the readers to the February, 1980 (Vol. 28, #8) issue of the Bulletin to save space and repetition.

Robert Taylor, forester, (sixteen years tenure with the Livingston Development Corporation) and now a foreman, left his home in Lothian at 1000 GMT in a Forestry Department van, to inspect young trees to the North of the town near highway M8. As he could not drive the van all the way due to the density of trees, he left it on the side of the roadway and proceeded on foot.

Mr. Taylor, accompanied by his dog—walked the rest of the way, and at about 10:15 he rounded a corner in the forest path (100 meters from the road but out of sight of it) and came upon a strange sight.

Before him was a rounded object with a rim-like appendage (according to Journal of Transient Aerial Phenomena) not unlike a circular.

At first the smaller objects were not in evidence, according to Taylor. The larger object was hovering above the ground, neither moving nor making any sound. The "thing" was dark grey with a texture similar to that of sand-paper. It appeared to become transparent in one area or another, seemingly, to Taylor, to "camouflage" itself. The "craft" was estimated to be twenty feet (six meters) in diameter.

Taylor said he stood, amazed, and stared at the object, then two small objects (apparently coming from under the large object) "rushed" toward him. They had a colour and texture similar to that of the "parent" object, but were outfitted with appendages. They rolled on a horizontal axis and made a "plopping" noise as the "legs" made contact with the ground.

Upon reaching him, these objects each attached itself to one (each) of his trouser legs, just below the pockets on the sides. Taylor felt them tug him toward the large object and at the same time, he said, he was nearly suffocated by a strong acrid smell which he compared with that of burning automobile brake linings and which he felt came from the "things".

Taylor became aware that he was being dragged forward and

his boots were scraping on the ground, before he lost consciousness, and fell forward and laid face downwards.

When Taylor regained consciousness, the objects were gone, but his dog was with him. He tried to speak to her but found he had lost his voice. He tried to stand but his legs would not support him, so he crawled approximately 90 meters (300 ft.) back up the trail toward his van, and then unsteadily half crawled and half staggered the rest of the 430 meters to his van. There, he attempted to contact his headquarters via two-way radio but was unsuccessful because of his voice.

Taylor then attempted to back the van up the track but unfortunately he ran off the track onto soft ground and could not get it out. Using short cuts through woods and fields, he walked the remaining 1600 meters back to his home, arriving at 11:30 A.M. During his walk between his van and his home his voice returned.

Upon seeing her husband's state when he arrived home, Mrs. Taylor assumed he had been attacked and started to call the police, but Taylor stopped her and had her call Mr. Malcolm Drummond, the head of the Forestry Department and his superior. Drummond immediately went to the Taylor residence and he and Taylor went back to the scene of the encounter where they found strange holes in the ground which Taylor said had not been there before that morning. Mrs. Taylor had noticed some unaccountable tears in his trousers in the areas where Taylor claimed the small objects had attached themselves.

Mr. Taylor was later examined by his Doctor who found only a "grase" (scrape?) on his chin and on his thigh. The Doctor sent him to the Bangour hospital for a skull X-ray but Taylor checked himself out before this was accomplished.

The following excerpts were taken from the "Journal of Transient Aerial Phenomena":

"The ground marks were of two types. First, there were two isolated ladder type "tracks" about 2.5 m long and the same distance apart. Each "rung" of the ladder, was 2 or 3 cm wide and deep, and about 30 cm long, and the area of grass between each "rung" was evenly flattened, but not as deeply as the "rungs". Although the "tracks" appear to be impressions made by a heavy object, the indentations were only in the grass; they did not alter the ground profile under the grass as they would have done if subjected to a heavy weight. The grass blades were each folded and formed to follow the outline of a rectangular indentations."

"Secondly there were 40 holes surrounding the "tracks". These holes all exposed fresh earth and were tapered from a maximum width of about 10 cm, but at an angle as shown, The angle was fairly shallow; about 30° to the horizontal. A remarkable feature was the fact that the direction of the angle of the holes was consistent and always in line with the next hole in line. Two distinct and related sets of holes can be detected, and it is clear that one set of holes proceeds clock-wise, while the other proceeds anticlock-wise, and that they are in tandem between the "tracks". In some cases, blades of grass surrounding the edge of a hole were sheared off."

"No grass was scorched. The marks were measured and recorded by the local police the same day, and the area fenced off by the Forestry Department. The marks were photographed by Alastair Sutherland (a friend of a member of the Forestry Department) and by me, the following day."

"Robert Taylor's clothes (including the trousers) were taken by the police for forensic examination. Only the trousers and his long underpants showed anything unusual. The tears on each leg of the trousers, which are made of navy blue serge. The right leg tear is about 65 cm up from the bottom of the leg, while the left tear is about 76 cm up."

UFO with Two Occupants Hovers over Man's Car

Full Report/Article

The occurrence took place on Mogford Road south of town shortly after 9 P.M., according to his interviews with the San Antonio man. The man was driving to a nearby store when he noticed a strange amber-coloured object rise rapidly from a grove of trees about 900 yards away.

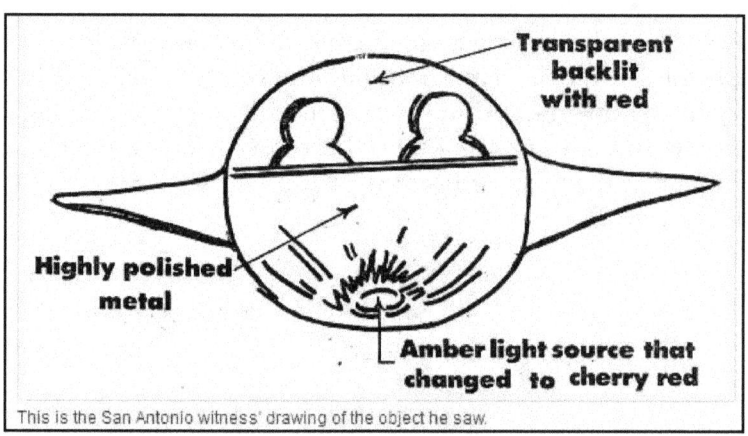

This is the San Antonio witness' drawing of the object he saw.

Date 1975
Location San Antonio, Texas, United States

The object then streaked toward the pickup truck "at a terrific rate of speed" as the light on the front of [he vehicle changed from amber to bright, cherry red. "When the craft got directly over the top of my pickup the lights went completely out and the engine was dead," the man said.

"As I was trying to get out of the pickup I thought it was a chopper passing on top of me, at first," he said.

"Then when they hovered over the top of me and I got a good look at it. I knew it was no chopper. I thought to myself, 'that's got to be a UFO,'" the man reported.

He said the craft was globular with a sort of shelf-like projection encircling the transparent upper section.

The bottom of the vehicle was highly polished metal and had the cherry red light apparently mounted onwards the front of the craft.

The UFO hovered over the truck for between 10 and 20 seconds and the man got a good look inside. The two creatures were not over five feet tall with tight, firm skin, he said

"They were bald, with long prominent ears and a long nose. Their eyes did not appear very plainly; they just looked like slits," he told the investigator.

The investigator speculates that the slits could have been lids or protective membranes to protect their eyes against glare.

Their skin "was not like our skin, it appeared to me to look sort of like sharkskin, sort of a grey colour," the witness reported.

"There was no motor noise -during the time it was over my truck, just a whirring (shriek) of wind. It was very loud, it sounded to me like a cyclone." ho said.

When the craft left it "look off straight up. There was a terrible thrust that buffeted my pickup and then it vanished almost instantly," the man said. "II was just like turning off a light bulb."

He noticed a strong odour like burning copper or electrical wiring while the craft hovered over his truck. The odour lingered for several days, he said. '

The man also reported eye strain from the intense red light, the report notes.

"I feel like they got a look at me. and maybe got my picture or something," the man told the investigator.

The report notes that he was familiar with the type of aircraft seen in San Antonio and discounts any possibility of the craft being a helicopter or other conventional plane.

Occupant Encounter in Argentina

Full Report/Article

On Sunday, October 28, 1973, in the first hour of the morning, truck driver Dionisio Llanca had a fantastic experience. Dionisio, a calm and quiet bachelor arrived at a hospital in Bahia Blanca in a state of total amnesia. Three days later as he regained his memory he related his extraordinary experience - - a night encounter on route H3 with a flying saucer and beings that talked with "chillidos" and who took a sample of his blood.

Date October 28, 1973
Location Bahia Blanca, Argentina

Dionisio Llanca got up late on Saturday, October 27, 1973 and put on old pants, shirt and dark sweater and lounged about the modest painted cottage on Calle Chubut, only ten minutes from the centre of Bahia Blanca. He ate lunch early and napped during the siesta period because he would have to drive all night long.

He arose about 6:00 P.M. and watched a television serial, which it should be noted was realistic and direct, and without fantastic elements. About 10:00 P.M. He ate a dinner of beef, salad, and two glasses of Cepita, a non-alcoholic beverage, with his uncle Enrique Ruiz. A few minutes after midnight Llanca said goodbye to his uncle and got into his truck, a Dodge 600, loaded with construction material to be delivered to Rio Gallegos, a two day trip. After 12 years of driving the eyes become accustomed to observing conditions, even in the shadow of the street. He discovered that the right rear tire was low. He was of a mind to change it but decided to leave instead. When he left the house it was 12:30. Sunday had already begun. The truck began to roll down route #3. The tire got lower and there was nothing to do but change it. Dionisio regretted not having changed it at the ESSO service station on Calle Don Bosco where he stopped at 15 minutes to 01:00 to get gasoline. Now he would have to get out on the dark and desolate shoulder in the cold of the morning and change it. It was now 01:15 and he was removing tools, wrenches and jack with no one to help. He began changing the tire. "I braked the truck on the shoulder, got down, took out the jack and the tools and began to change the tire. The road was completely deserted. All at once the road was illuminated with an intense yellow light that seemed to be about 2,000 meters distant. Because of the colour I thought that they might be the headlights of a Pugeot and continued with my work. A few seconds passed and I had my shoulder to the light but it became so bright that it lighted the whole area. Now the light had changed to a bluish colour similar to an electric arc welder. I tried to get up but could not rise; I had no strength, and a strange thing - - my legs would not respond. I was on my knees. I wanted to get up and look towards the woods that grew along one side of the road. Then I saw a great thing in the form of a plate suspended in the air at some seven meters altitude, and three persons at my shoulders looking at me. I tried once more to get up but could not. The paralysis became total and I could not even talk. The three beings stood looking at me for a long time, perhaps five minutes. They were two men and a woman. The woman was between the two men. I believed it was a woman because of the form of the breast and the long hair, blonde, reaching to the middle of her shoulders. The men were also blond with shorter hair in back. The three were about the same height, one meter and 70 or 75 centimeters, and dressed in the same manner: single piece smoky gray coverall suits well fitted to the figure, yellow boots and long gloves reaching to the middle of the arm of the same colour. They had no belts, nor weapons, nor helmets nor anything else. Their faces were like ours except for high foreheads and elongated eyes, like the Japanese and a little tilted. They talked among themselves in a language impossible for me to understand. They had no vocal inflections but sounded like a...... like a radio badly tuned with chirps and buzzes. One of them grabbed me by the neck of my sweater and lifted me firmly but without violence. I tried to talk but my voice would not come out. While the one held me up another put an apparatus in the base of my index finger on the left hand. They looked closely at the apparatus. It was like a razor but had a small tube. They applied it to me for several seconds. It did not hurt. When they left I had two drops of blood on my finger. I believe I then passed out because I can remember nothing else."

Dionisio could not remember when he a-woke. The time is calculated to be between 2 and 3 A. M. on Sunday. When he opened his eyes he was among the rail cars in the yard of the Sociedad Rural de Bahia Blanca, exactly 9 kilometers 600 meters from the point where the encounter took place. He could remember nothing, not even his name, nor the episode, nor the truck, nor his home. He was nauseated and cold. He began walking toward the road guided by the lights of the vehicles. Recently, on the 30th when he awoke in a bed in the Municipal Hospital of Bahia Blanca he remembered the experience in detail. His clothes were intact, folded in the drawers of the bed. He felt a desire to smoke and to know what time it was. He went to his clothes and discovered that his watch was missing, and also his cigarette lighter and cigarettes in a metal box were missing. The pockets of his pants still contained the 150 thousand pesos that he carried upon leaving home. He asked about his truck which worried him more than the UFO and its occupants. He was told that the police had found it parked on a shoulder in Villa Bordeu, some 18 kilometers from Bahia Blanca, with the jack in place and one tire ready to change. His papers in the glove compartment had not been disturbed.

It is still a mystery concerning what occurred between the time Dionisio awakened among the rail cars, some 10 kilometers from where the encounter took place, and the time when he was treated by Doctor Ricardo Smirnoff at the hospital. "I am a forensic surgeon. I had rotating duty on Sunday the 28th. About 9:30 Dr. Altaperro at the Spanish Hospital called me and said that he had a curious case. I arrived at the hospital about 10:15 and saw a young man of about 25 or 26 years of age in a state of total amnesia. He could remember nothing of his past. He did not know who he was, where he was born, who his parents were or anything about his past. He cried continually and asked what town he was in. The doctor told me that a man had left him at the hospital after encountering him wandering in the centre of the city, like a robot, and asking everyone he met where a police box was. At first he thought that he had had an automobile accident on the road. He changed this as he had no injuries. When I touched his head or came near his hand he drew back instinctively as though it would produce pain. He had a bad headache in the right parietal temporal area. I notified the police and had him admitted to the Municipal Hospital."

Dionisio Llanca is a simple, almost primitive man. In two days of interviews he remained withdrawn and did not even smile. He is serious with a remote sense of humour. One of the doctors characterized him as "innocent." When he is asked what he thinks about UFOs, he says "Nothing, It doesn't interest me." In reality, there are few subjects that -Interest Dionisio except his town, his parents and his work. He does not like to think about the events of that night.

UFO with Humanoid Encountered by Two Forestry Workers in Finland

Full Report/Article

On Friday, February 5, 1971, two young men from Kinnula. Petter Aliranta (21) and Esko Juhani Sneck (18), were working in the woods of the village of Kangaskyla in Kinnula, near the borders of the counties of Middle Finland and Vaasa. At about 3.00 P.M. they were about to end their work, for the cloudy day was slowly turning dark. Aliranta had just turned off his motor saw, when he suddenly noticed a strange metallic-looking object at tree-top

Date February 5, 1971
Location Kinnula, Finland

level which was descending straight down. It had the shape of two saucers on top of each other and was about 5 meters in diameter. At the bottom of the vehicle there were four thin (5-10 cms.) landing feet, more than 2 meters long. Within a few moments the object descended in a small opening between the trees, about 15 meters away from Aliranta and Sneck. The last-mentioned, however, did not notice what was going on at this time as he was still busy cutting branches off a tree with his motor saw.

During the descent, a round opening appeared in the centre of the underpart of the UFO, and from this, immediately the vehicle had settled firmly on the ground, a strange little being glided down. It actually did glide down those two meters to the snow-covered ground; there was no normal falling movement. After this, the being started approaching Aliranta. Its movements were very stiff and the steps short. The being looked like a space-man, or robot, and was less than 1 meter tall, perhaps 90 cms. The body was covered with a one-piece suit of a green colour. The head had the same cover, and in the middle of it was a sort of lens facing forwards. The hands were round at the tips and no fingers could be seen. The "boots'" at the feet were a uniform part of the dress, and green as well.

The humanoid seemed to move in a strange way on top of the snow surface; it did not go down into the deep snow as one would have expected. As this entity was slowly but steadily advancing towards Aliranta, he started his motor saw and began to approach the strange walker with motor saw in hand. At this point, Esko Sneck also became aware of the strange happenings; the turning on of the motor saw had made him turn around to see what Aliranta was up to.

"The little green man" and Aliranta were approaching each other, the distance between them now less than 10 meters. Suddenly the being turned around and started eventually to go back towards the saucer. This made Aliranta braver, and he hurried to catch the humanoid. Within the saucer, other entities were now visible; there were three "windows" on the topside of the vehicle (about 1 meter wide) and through one on the right side three moving forms were visible, humanlike, although no features or details could be seen.

As Petter Aliranta was about to get hold of the humanoid, when about 3 meters from the saucer, it rose into the air in a strange way, floating towards the opening from which it had come. The humanoid having risen to more than 1 meter above the ground, Aliranta reached out quickly and grabbed hold of the heel of the right "boot" with his bare right hand. However, he had lo let go of the foot right away as it burned like a hot iron (the wounds caused by the burning on the thumb, forefinger and inside of the hand were still clearly visible two months later). At the same time, Aliranta automatically took a couple of steps backwards, so the entity was able to glide back into the craft undisturbed.

The moment the humanoid had got into the saucer, the latter started to give a slight humming or buzzing sound, and it slowly started to ascend from the ground. Aliranta felt a weak gust of air at this moment, but no smoke or smell could be detected, nor any light phenomenon (there were no lights visible on or in the vehicle during the incident). As the saucer rose upwards the round opening at the bottom closed (but the landing feet kept their position) and within some fifteen seconds the whole object had disappeared into the sky.

According to the eye-witnesses, the visit of this strange craft lasted at least three minutes. After the saucer had disappeared the men could not talk, for they were too amazed by the whole incident. They felt stiff all over and had some difficulty in moving, especially Petter Aliranta. It took them close on one hour before they were able to walk away from the woods. Before they left they had a closer look at the markings left in the snow, evidence of this incredible happening.

At the end of each landing foot there had been a round plate. These plates had penetrated the full depth of the snow cover (then about 40 cms.), leaving four round prints (about 35 cms. across) in an even square with a side of about 2 meters. Within this square the snow had melted some 5-10 cms on the surface. The footsteps left by the humanoid were also clearly visible. They were small (15 cms.) and quite circular in shape. The strides were all along the same length (even those made during the chase): about 20 cms.

During the course of the investigation no details appeared of anything which could have made the story of these two men questionable.

UFO and Occupants seen near Cowichan Hospital in BC, Canada

Full Report/Article

It was turning five in the morning on New Year's Day 1970, when Miss Doreen Kendall, a practical nurse at the Cowichan District Hospital on Vancouver Island, noticed that one of the elderly patients in her ward was restless. Deciding the patient was too warm, she went to a window and parted the drapes to let in a little air.

Date January 1, 1970
Location Duncan, British Columbia, Canada

"Just as I pulled the drapes a brilliant light hit me in the eyes," she said. "It was still dark outside, but about 60 feet away right above the children's ward to my left there was this object so big and bright I could see everything clearly."

"The object was circular and had what I guess you would call a top and bottom. The bottom was silvery, like metal, and was shaped like a bowl. There was a string of bright lights around it like a necklace. The top was a dome made of something like glass. It was lit up from inside and I could see right into it."

Continuing her account in question-and-answer form, Miss Kendall told me there were two male-like figures in the craft, one behind the other, facing to her right away from the hospital. The one in front appeared taller, or perhaps was positioned higher, than the other. Their heads were encased in close-fitting dark material.

As she watched with intense curiosity, yet completely unfrightened - "I never felt so peaceful in all my life. I wish I could have talked to them" - she became aware of seeing more of the interior of the craft and realized it was tilting. In a moment she could see to a point just below their knees and noticed they were standing in front of what looked like stools.

"They looked like fine, tall, well-built men," she said. "They were dressed in tight-fitting suits of the same material that covered their heads but their hands were bare and I noticed how human they looked. Their flesh seemed just like ours."

Intrigued as she was by the appearance of the two figures, Miss Kendall found her interest centreed on what looked like an instrument panel facing the one in front.

"The man in front was staring at the panel as if something very important was going on, and I wondered if they might have had mechanical trouble. I even thought they might have landed on the roof of the hospital and then had trouble taking off."

She described the panel as a very large one, taking up almost half the interior of the object and reaching nearly to the top of the dome. The instruments, if that is what they were, seemed to be inset in the chrome-like metal of the panel and there was a variety of sizes.

The total sight was so absorbing that at first Miss Kendall's thoughts were lost to everything else, and for a moment she forgot Mrs. Frieda Wilson, a registered nurse, was in the same room.

"Then when I did think of it, I guess I hesitated. I felt I mustn't make a noise or do anything that would break the trend of what was happening."

At this point, almost as if her thoughts were being read, she saw the figure in the rear turn slowly and face squarely in her direction.

"He seemed to look right at me but I couldn't see his face. It was covered by a darkish material that looked softer than the rest of his suit. I'm sure he saw me because then he touched the other man on the back. When he did this, the man in front reached down and took hold of something like a lever beside him. I'll never forget how deliberately he did it. He pushed it back and forth and the saucer, or whatever you'd call it, started to circle slowly, still close to the building, in an anticlockwise direction."

The motion seemed to break the spell for Miss Kendall, for then she remembered Mrs. Wilson was there and called her over.

Later I spoke separately to Mrs. Wilson, who said, "I noticed Miss Kendall standing at the window and wondered what she was looking at. In fact, I was just going to see when she beckoned to me, and then I saw this great big light over the patio outside the children's ward. I'd say it was quite a bit larger than a car. (By the estimate of both witnesses, the object spanned a width of about five windows of the children's ward. This gave it a diameter of at least 50 feet.) It looked circular in shape and the far side seemed to be higher than the side near us. It was moving around slowly and then it started to move away. I didn't really see any top or bottom to it. It was all just tremendously bright."

Milakovic Family Encounter, Hanbury, England

Full Report/Article

Figures Seen on UFO

The small, dank mining town of Hednesford, Staffordshire, England, lies near the southern end of Cannock Chase. Mr. and Mrs. Milin Milakovic and their 11 children live at 432 Cannock Road. On the afternoon of November 20, 1968, the Yugoslavian couple and their 11-year old son, Slavic, left Hednesford on a house-hunting trip. They journeyed through the English countryside to Rugeley,

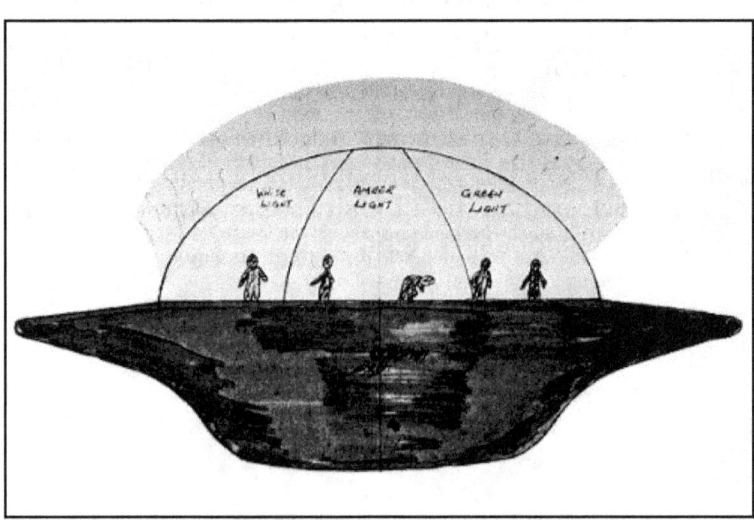

Date November 20, 1968
Location Hanbury, England, United Kingdom

Abbots Bromley, and stopped at Hanbury to view Hanbury Hall.

Hanbury, on the Staffordshire-Derbyshire border, is midway between Uttoexter and Burton-on-Trent. Three and one-half miles to the northwest is Central Workshop 32 R.E.M.E., an army installation. Two miles to the northwest is a Royal Air Force station, used as an ammunition dump "and there are very vague rumours that nuclear weapons are stored there." Three miles to the south is a World War IT airfield, used by the Ind Coope brewery firm for light aircraft.

On the road home, the Milakovics stopped just outside Hanbury to look at an old house for sale. As they continued on, dusk was rapidly approaching. It was between 5:30 and 5:45 P.M.

The couple saw a rabbit scurry across the road, followed by a number of other rabbits from a hedge on the left side of the road. Glancing to the left, the witnesses saw a brilliant object in the field. Milakovic stopped the car as the UFO rose slowly and flew over the car. The couple got out of the automobile and watched as the object moved over a field on the right side of the road toward a house about 100 yards away. As it got over the house, it stopped, hovered, and quivered "like a jelly."

Doris Milakovic said that the air temperature appeared considerably warmer as the UFO flew overhead, but, as it moved on, the temperature dropped. She also said that the object looked "as wide as the house."

For approximately five minutes, Mrs. Milakovic, her husband and son saw what appeared to be several humanoid figures walking across the bright top of the UFO. Intermittently, "some of the figures were seen to bend down as though looking at something in the part of the object below the rim. ... ."

Then the object began moving up in a "pulsating or jerky" movement- Its light intensity greatly increased and Milakovic felt his eyes were burning.

Thoroughly frightened, Milakovic, normally a brave man, pushed his wife and son into the car and sped away from the scene.

N. M. H. Turner and W. Daniels investigated the report.

Valensole, France Landing (Maurice Masse Case)

Full Report/Article

A Farmer is Detained by Aliens in France

On July 1, 1965, at about 5:45 in the morning, in the region of Valensole, Basses Alpes, France, farmer Maurice Masse was inspecting his field of lavender when he heard a whistling sound, then noticed an egg-shaped object with six thin legs and a central pedestal standing nearby. Masse later said the object was about the size of a small car, and he could see two seats inside an open

Date July 1, 1965
Location Valensole, Basses Alpes, France

doorway. At the same time, he also saw two "small boys," humanoid-looking beings less than four feet tall, dressed in grayish-green one-piece coveralls. Masse reported that they appeared to be gathering handfuls of his lavender. He said they had large, hairless heads, smooth white skin, large slanted eyes, pointed chins and small mouths with no lips. Masse heard them make soft gurgling sounds, as if communicating. When he approached, one of them pointed a small "tube" at Masse, which immediately immobilized him where he stood. He remained conscious, watching as they finished their task and then entered the egg-shaped object, which rose off the ground, moved quickly away, then suddenly disappeared a few moments later. Masse was left standing paralyzed in his field, but regained his mobility about fifteen minutes later.

Masse reported his encounter in detail to local authorities, including the mayor of Valensole, his parish priest and the gendarmerie. The site was thoroughly inspected, and symmetrical marks were found in the ground exactly where Masse said the legs of the object had been. It was later discovered that lavender would not grow on that spot for a period of ten years. Four days after the encounter, Masse began to experience bouts of profound drowsiness which caused him to require more than twelve hours of sleep every day for the next several months. Despite his reported immobilization by the humanoid beings, and his later health difficulties, Masse said he had a positive feeling about his encounter. Masse was well-known and highly respected in his community, and all the local authorities who examined his claims reached the conclusion that he was telling the truth.

Socorro/Zamora UFO Incident

Full Report/Article

The experience of Lonnie Zamora on April 24, 1964 stands as one of the most profound UFO events in the modern history of the phenomena. To this day it remains a case in which all the facts involved support the witnesses claims and it is this kind of case that makes the UFO phenomenon such an enduring mystery. Lonnie Zamora saw a highly unusual device of unknown origin, what can only be described as a "craft" of some kind, and he reported seeing what he believes were occupants. Despite the controversy which often surrounds the subject of UFOs, the incident at Socorro remains an example of what the UFO phenomenon is, in fact, all about.

Date April 24, 1964
Location Socorro, New Mexico, United States

The following information is based on facts I have gathered from various sources including conversations in person and by telephone with Mr. Lonnie Zamora. This is not intended to be a complete report on Lonnie Zamora's experience, but is intended to provide a source for some resh details about the case and to clarify others. More than anything else I have made every effort to ensure that what is here is the truth. I also owe a great deal of gratitude to Mr. Ray Stanford, one of the most thorough and knowledgeable investigators I have met. He arrived in Socorro within four days of the incident and authored the definitive book on Zamora's experience and the subsequent investigation. I recommend it to anyone seriously interested in this case and in the subject of UFO's in general. "Socorro Saucer" in a Pentagon Pantry" is available in major libraries but can be obtained from the author.

Socorro is a small town located about an hours drive south of Albuquerque, New Mexico . In April 1964, Lonnie Zamora was a police officer with the town and late in the afternoon on April, 24th he had just dropped his pursuit of a speeding car to go check on what he thought might have been an explosion on the outskirts of town. Thinking that a small shack containing dynamite might have exploded, he made his way up a rough embankment and then moved slowly along a narrow gravel road that wound beside a small arroyo (a shallow dry gully). From this first more distant vantage point he saw what he thought might have been an overturned car down in the arroyo and radioed back to his headquarters that he was proceeding to check out this 'vehicle'. It was from here that he saw what he described as possibly two children or small adults, and he noted that one appeared startled at his approach and seemed to "jump somewhat".

He moved further along the gravel road and finally stopped his car at the point where he believed he had previously seen the vehicle in the arroyo. It was at this point that he heard what he later could describe as several loud "thumps" or "slams", similar to metal hitting metal. As he left his patrol car and proceeded towards the gulley, he had not gone more than a few steps before he had a full view of an elongated oval shaped object on "girder-like" legs. In that instant a loud roar and bluish flame shot out of the underside of the object and it began to rise. Zamora did not hesitate...he hit the ground thinking it was about to explode, then got up running and jumped down on the other side of the gravel road. He heard a whirring noise and watched the object rise up out of the arroyo, the legs he saw moments before were no longer apparent. He noted that the object had risen to perhaps 20 feet above the bottom of the gulley when suddenly the sound stopped completely. There was no more flame visible and he watched as the now-silent vehicle moved off parallel to the terrain picking up speed as it left the area. He watched it move off into the distance and it eventually disappeared from view.

Almost immediately upon the object having left the area, State Police Sergeant Sam Chavez arrived having overheard Zamora who had radioed wildly to his dispatcher hoping that someone else might be able to see the object. Together they noted the evidence left in the arroyo...a half burned bush, four angular impressions in the sandy soil where the "legs" had been, and several small footprints and other impressions.

From an oil painting based on photographs taken of the actual landing site. The image portrays the object just as it began to lift off and from a viewpoint near where Mr. Zamora reportedly stood. Mr. Zamora has seen this illustration and stated that it is a good representation of what he observed, though he felt that the "legs" might have been extended slightly further than is portrayed. The dimensions presented however are taken from both the witnesses description and the exact measurements provided by investigators of the impressions in the soil.

Ever since the first report that Zamora had seen some type of symbol on the side of the craft there had been some confusion about just what that symbol was. He had drawn and described this symbol to several people soon after the incident, and what appeared to be discrepancies in the description had arisen from various sources. There does appear to be some support for believing that the symbol that was widely circulated early on may have actually been a variation of the actual one. The idea that a substitute might have been circulated by the investigative personnel from the Air Force or other governmental agencies as a way to guard against copycat reports has some merit. Though the actual shape may not be ultimately important to the overall case I did make an effort to try to obtain an honest description of just what Zamora saw. In one of our telephone conversations he clarified to me that he had never been told -not- to relate the actual shape and he gave me a description which I realized was slightly different from what I had heard and seen before. I was curious about this and shortly afterward I sent him several pages of small sketches which covered various details of his sighting. I included several variations of this symbol including one that matched what I had seen in other places and one that matched what I thought he had described to me. I asked him to merely place a check mark by whichever sketch matched his recollection. Below are several sections of the sheets I sent him, and his check marks are visible. But on the section showing the symbols, he was nice enough to actually redraw what he had seen.

Of all the evidence that could be presented to support the contention that what Lonnie Zamora saw was something totally unexplained, perhaps nothing is more compelling than this brief article. It appeared in the formerly classified CIA publication entitled "Studies in Intelligence" from the fall of 1966. It was written by Hector Quintanilla, Jr., the former head of the Air Force's Project Bluebook.

It gives a history and methodology of the Air Force's investigation of UFO's, and after presenting many of the prosaic explanations that had been encountered, he concluded his article with a synopsis of a "Policeman's Report" in which he described the Socorro incident. One short quote from this article in itself makes a profound statement about the reality of some UFO reports.

"There is no doubt that Lonnie Zamora saw an object which left quite an impression on him. There is also no question about Zamora"s reliability. He is a serious police officer, a pillar of his church, and a man well versed in recognizing airborne vehicles in his area. He is puzzled by what he saw, and frankly, so are we. This is the best-documented case on record, and still we have been unable, in spite of thorough investigation, to find the vehicle or other stimulus that scared Zamora to the point of panic."

Eagle River Close Encounter (Man given 'Pancakes' by UFO Occupants)

Full Report/Article

Wisconsin's strangest close encounter of the third kind must surely be the incident during which Joe Simonton was given three pancakes by "Italian-looking" aliens.

Date April 18, 1961
Location Eagle River, Wisconsin, United States

A close encounter of the third kind is an actual meeting between humans and extraterrestrials, and Simonton's is easily the state's best known. Despite the unlikely manner in which the story unfolded, the episode survived a rigorous assessment by the U.S. Air Force and is carried in their files as "unexplained."

In 1961, Joe Simonton was a plumber; auctioneer and Santa Claus - annually, for the Eagle River Chamber of Commerce. He reported his age as 55 or 60, depending on the interviewer: At 11 A.M., April 18, Simonton was having a late breakfast when he heard a sound like that of a jet being throttled back, something like the sound of "knobby tires on wet pavement." He went into the yard and saw a flying saucer drop out of the sky and hover over his farm. It was silver and "brighter than chrome," 12 feet in height and 30 feet in diameter. On one edge were what appeared to be exhaust pipes, 6 or 7 inches in diameter.

The disc landed and a hatch opened. Inside were three dark-skinned aliens, each about 5 feet tall and weighing about 125 pounds. They appeared to be between 25 and 30 years old and were dressed in dark blue or black knit uniforms with turtleneck tops, and helmet-like caps. They were clean-shaven, Simonton said, and "Italian-looking."

The aliens did not speak in his presence, but they had a silvery jug with two handles, heavier than aluminum but lighter than steel, about a foot high. It seemed to be made out of the same material as the craft. Simonton said it was "a beautiful thing, a Thermos jug-like bottle quite unlike any jug I have ever seen here [on Earth]."

Through ESP or something, Simonton got the idea that the aliens wanted water. He left the visitors, filled the jug from the water pump in his basement, then returned to the craft and gave the jug back. To do this, he had to brace himself against the UFO's hull and stretch up. From the subsequent Air Force report: "Looking into the [saucer] he saw a man 'cooking' on some kind of flameless cooking appliance." The alien was preparing pancakes.

The interior of the UFO was dull black, even the three "extremely beautiful" instrument panels, and had the appearance of wrought iron. The contrast between the dark interior and shiny exterior so fascinated Simonton that he later said that he "would love to have a room painted in the same way."

In return for the water, one of the aliens - the only one with narrow red trim on his trousers - presented Simonton with three of the pancakes, hot from the griddle. As he did so, the alien touched his own forehead, apparently a salute in thanks to Simonton for his help. Simonton saluted back. Each of the pancakes was roughly 3 inches in diameter and perforated with small holes.

The head alien then connected a line or belt to a hook in his clothing and the hatch closed. The saucer rose about 20 feet and took off to the south, at a 45 degree angle. Its rise left a blast of air that tossed the tops of nearby pine trees. The craft took only two seconds to disappear from view.

Simonton ate one of the pancakes, ostensibly in the interest of science. "It tasted like cardboard," he told the Associated Press. The other two pancakes he gave to Vilas County Judge Frank Carter, a local UFO enthusiast. Carter, who called the aliens "saucernauts" ("I prefer Italians"), said he believed Simonton's story since he could not think of any way in which the farmer might profit from a hoax. Carter's son, Colyn, today a lawyer in Eagle River, told me, "I recall as a youngster that my dad took it very seriously."

Judge Carter sent the pancakes to what was then the country's top investigative group, the National Investigations Committee on Aerial Phenomena (NICAP). They refused the opportunity to check it out. That put a damper on Judge Carter's plans; he had wanted to hold a seminar on the incident.

By this time, Simonton said, he was "irked by reporters making fun of the situation and laughing."

In response to all this, the Air Force dispatched its civilian UFO investigator, J. Allen Hynek. Hynek at the time was an astronomer at Northwestern University. He later became convinced that UFOs are real, and founded his own investigative agency, which took over NICAP's files after that group folded. Thanks to Hynek, a Northwestern University committee and the Air Force's Technical Intelligence Centre analyzed one of Simonton's pancakes and found it to be made of flour, sugar and grease; it was rumoured, however, that the wheat in the pancakes was of an unknown type.

The official Air Force assessment of it all said: This case is unexplained. "The only serious flaw in the story is the disappearance of the craft in 'two seconds.' The rest of the story did not contain any outrages to physical concepts," reads the report. Simonton "answered questions directly, did not contradict himself, insisted on the facts being exactly as he stated and refused to accept embellishments or modifications. He stated he was sure that we wouldn't believe him but that he didn't care whether he was believed. He stated simply that this happened and that was that."

The private Air Force response was unearthed after a little detective work. It comes from a UFO handbook for Air Force personnel, written by Lloyd Mallan and issued in a popular edition by Science and Mechanics Publishing Co. In the book, Mallan refers to "J.S., a highly regarded, much respected citizen of Eagle River, Wis. -- a small rural community noted for its attractiveness to tourists."

(Unless there are more space-pancake recipients in Eagle River than otherwise reported, we can safely see through Mallan's clever attempt at disguise and positively identify "J.S." as Joe Simonton.)

One Air Force investigator, according to Mallan, said that Simonton "appeared quite sincere to me, did not appear to be the perpetrator of a hoax." But an Air Force Aeronautical Systems Division psychiatrist believed that Simonton had suffered a hallucination and subsequent delusion. The Air Technical Intelligence Centre investigator said, "cases of this type could be injurious to the mental health of the individual if [he] became upset due to the experience. ...It was pointed out that experiences of this type, hallucinations followed by delusion, are not at all uncommon and especially in rural communities."

Additionally, according to Mallan, the Air Force took to heart an unsubstantiated rumour circulated by, among others, Raymond Palmer, a publisher of pulp flying-saucer and science-fiction magazines. Palmer reported to the Air Force his belief that Simonton had been hypnotized by an Eagle River real estate broker and was fed the pancake story so that he would repeat it and appear truthful. The motivation for this was economic, for the purpose of "a miniature Disneyland that is or was being built in the area."

To understand how incredible the rumour was, it is useful to look at the credibility of Palmer himself. One of his favourite theories was that flying saucers came from a secret hollow-Earth civilization ruled by a race called Detrimental Robots, which he abbreviated as "Deros." According to Palmer, the Deros manipulated humanity with their projected thought rays. Palmer's primary source -- actually, his only source -- was a Pennsylvania welder who drew upon "racial memory" for his accounts. (There apparently is no mention in Air Force files of the possibility that the Deros' thought-ray had been turned upon real estate agents, or Palmer, or even the Air Force, though I believe there is as much evidence for that as for an Eagle River Disneyland.)

But based on such sound "evidence," the Air Technical Intelligence Centre, which headquartered Air Force UFO investigations, let the matter drop. Publicly, it was a mystery. The classified reason, revealed to Mallan, was that the Air Force would not pursue the matter "due to the possibility of causing [Simonton] embarrassment which might prove injurious to his health." This was an uncharacteristic kindness on the part of the Air Force; they regularly had been dismissing reports from pilots - even their own - as misidentifications or, worse, hallucinations. "There are sufficient psychological explanations for reports not otherwise explainable," concluded the Psychology Branch of the Air Force's Aeromedical Laboratory in 1949. Pilots, police, professors, besides regular folks -- all nuts. In the 60's, though, for a brief, shining moment, the Air Force took on a human face and it its collective tongue, bending over backwards to carry the case of a part-time Santa and full-time chicken farmer as unexplained. Some may smell a conspiracy here.

As for Simonton himself, in the end he was left with a bitter taste in his mouth, and it wasn't from the pancakes. "I haven't been able to work for three weeks," he told United Press International. "I'm going to have to start making some money." He said that the next time he saw a flying saucer he would keep it to himself.

He lied. In 1970 Simonton was visited by Lee Alexander, a UFO enthusiast active in a Detroit-based investigative group. Simonton told Alexander that he had had more visits from the aliens, but he had not told anyone because of the way his first report had been received.

And that is all we know.

Father Gill / Papua New Guinea Sighting

Full Report/Article

In 1959 Papua New Guinea was still a territory of Australia. June of that year saw the spectacular sightings by Father William Gill, an Australian Anglican missionary, and 37 members of his Boianai mission. Gill made notes about the experience, which the media obtained. Stories appeared in August, causing a sensation. I have had two extended interviews with Reverend Gill and was impressed with his quiet and certain manner in relating the events. What follows comes from his own account of the affair.

Date June 26, 1959
Location Papua New Guinea

Only the day before the sighting, Gill had composed a letter to the Reverend David Durie, Acting Principal of Saint Aidan's College at Dogura, to accompany a report regarding a UFO sighting made by Stephen Moi, an assistant teacher at Gill's mission.

'Dear David, Have a look at this extraordinary data. I am almost convinced about the "visitation" theory. There have been quite a number of reports over the months, from reliable witnesses. The peculiar thing about these most recent reports is that the UFOs seem to be stationary at Boianai or to travel from Boianai. The Mount Pudi vicinity seems to be the hovering area. I myself saw a stationary white light twice on the same night on April 9, but in a different place each time.

I believe your students have also sighted one over Boianai. The Assistant District Officer, Bob Smith and Mr. Glover have all seen it, or similar ones on different occasions again, over Boianai, although I think the Baniara people said they watched it travel across the sky from our direction. I should think that this is the first time that the "saucer" has been identified as such.

'I do not doubt the existence of these "things" (indeed I cannot, now that I have seen one for myself) but my simple mind still requires scientific evidence before I can accept the from outer space theory. I am inclined to believe that probably many UFOs are more likely some form of electric phenomena, or perhaps something brought about by the atom bomb explosions, etc.

That Stephen should actually make out a saucer could be the work of the unconscious mind as it is very likely that at some time he has seen illustrations of some kind in a magazine, or it is very possible that saucers do exist, but it is only a 50/50 chance that they are not earth made, still less that they should carry men (more likely radio controlled), and it is still unproven that they are solids.

'It is all too difficult to understand for me; I prefer to wait for some bright boy to catch one to be exhibited in Martin Square. 'Please return this report as I have no copy and I want Nor, (Rev. Norman Crutwell) to have it. Yours, Doubting William Anglican Mission, Boianai. 27/6/59'

The events of the next day converted the Doubting William, as the next letter graphically indicates.

'Dear David,

Life is strange, isn't it? Yesterday I wrote you a letter, (which I still intend sending you) expressing opinions re: The UFOs. Now, less than twenty-four hours later I have changed my views somewhat. Last night we at Boianai experienced about four hours of UFO activity, and there is no doubt whatsoever that they are handled by beings of some kind. At times it was absolutely breathtaking. Here is the report. Please pass it round, but great care must be taken as I have no other, and this, like the one I made out re: Stephen, will be sent to Nor. I would appreciate it if you could send the lot back as soon as poss.

Cheers, Convinced Bill'

As indicated by his notes, Gill saw a bright white light in the north western sky. It appeared to be approaching the mission and hovering about 100 meters up. Eventually 38 people, including Gill, teachers Steven Gill Moi and Ananias Rarata, and Mrs Nessle Moi, gathered to watch the main UFO, which looked like a large, disc-shaped object. It was apparently solid and circular with a wide base and narrower upper deck. The object appeared to have four 'legs' underneath it. There also appeared to be about four 'panels' or 'portholes' on the side of the object, which seemed to glow a little brighter than the rest. At a number of intervals the object produced a shaft of blue light which shone upwards into the sky at an angle of about 45 degrees.

What looked like 'men' came out of the object, onto what seemed to be a deck on top of it. There were four men in all, occasionally two, then one, then three, then four. The shaft of blue light and the 'men' disappeared. The object then moved through some clouds. There were other UFO sightings during the night. Gill described the weather as variable sky scattered clouds to clear at first, becoming overcast after. He estimated the height of the clouds at about 600 meters. The first sighting over the sea, according to Rev. Gill, seemed to be about 150 meters above the water all times. The main UFO was clearly visible and seemed mostly stationary during the twenty-five minutes of observation.

Astonishingly, the aerial visitor put in a repeat performance the following night, June 27. Gill prepared another statement.

'Large UFO first sighted by Annie Laurie at 6 P.M. in apparently same position as last night (26/6/59) only seemed a little smaller, when W.B.G. saw it at 6.02 P.M. I called Ananias and several others and we stood in the open to watch it. Although the sun had set it was still quite light for the following fifteen minutes. We watched figures appear on top four of them, no doubt that they are human. Possibly the same object that I took to be the "Mother" ship last night. Two smaller UFOs were seen at the same time, stationary.

One above the hills west, another over-head. On the large one two of the figures seemed to be doing something near the centre of the deck, were occasionally bending over and raising their arms as though adjusting or "setting up" something (not visible). One figure seemed to be standing looking down at us (a group of about a dozen). I stretched my arm above my head and waved. To our surprise the figure did the same. Ananias waved both arms over his head then the two outside figures did the same. Ananias and self began waving our arms and all four now seemed to wave back. There seemed to be no doubt that our movements were answered. All mission boys made audible gasps (of either joy or surprise, perhaps both).

'As dark was beginning to close in, I sent Eric Kodawara for a torch and directed a series of long dashes towards the UFO. After a minute or two of this, the UFO apparently acknowledged by making several wavering motions back and forth. Waving by us was repeated and this followed by more flashes of torch, then the UFO began slowly to become bigger, apparently coming in our direction. It ceased after perhaps half a minute and came no further. After a further two or three minutes the figures apparently lost interest in us for they disappeared "below" deck. At 6.25 P.M. two figures re-appeared to carry on with whatever they were doing before the interruption. The blue spotlight came on for a few seconds twice in succession.'

Gill has described how he and the mission people called out to the men, even shouting at them, and beckoned them to descend, but there was no response beyond what has already been noted. Two smaller UFOs higher up remained stationary. By 6.30 P.M. the scene had remained largely unchanged, and Gill records that he went to dinner. Subsequently critics were to question this, why would someone walk away from such an extraordinary sight? 'I'm always asked this question,' Gill has said, 'either in puzzlement or with a sneer.

Having had about four hours of this sight on Friday night, we were not nearly so interested when it returned on Saturday night, especially after we were unable to persuade it to land. You must also keep in mind that there was nothing eerie or other worldly about any of this. It was all so ordinary, as ordinary as a Ford car. It looked a perfectly normal sort of object, an earth made object. I realised, of course, that some people might think of this as a flying saucer but I took it to be some kind of hovercraft the Americans or even the Australians had built.

The figures inside looked perfectly human. In fact, I thought they were human, that if we got them to land we would find the pilots to be ordinary earthmen in military uniforms and we would have dinner with them.

At 7.00 P.M. the 'No. 1 UFO' was still present, although it appeared somewhat smaller. The group of observers went to church for evensong. After evensong, visibility was very limited with the sky covered in cloud. Nothing else was seen that evening. At 10.40 P.M., a very penetrating, 'ear splitting' explosion woke up people on the station. It sounded like it had come from just outside the window of the mission house. Gill felt it did not sound like a thunderclap. Nothing had been seen, but the whole sky was overcast. Other less compelling activity occurred the following night. Then it seemed the Boianai visitors had gone. But the controversy had just begun.

Reverend Gill was at the time of his sightings already scheduled to return to Australia. This presented civilian groups with an excellent opportunity to assess the credibility of the reports.

All investigators found Gill to be very impressive. This led one of the leading civilian groups, the Victorian Flying Saucer Research Society, to view the Gill reports as constituting the most remarkable testimony of intensive UFO activity ever reported to civilian investigators. They were unique because for the first time credible witnesses had reported the presence of humanoid beings associated with UFOs. The major civilian groups of the day, in a spirit of new found cooperation inspired by the significance of the Boianai observations, distributed copies of Gill's sighting report to all members of the House of Representatives of Australia's federal parliament.

A letter accompanied the report, signed by the presidents of the participating civilian UFO groups, urging members of parliament to press the Minister for Air for a statement about the attitude Air Force Intelligence had to the New Guinea reports.

On November 24, 1959 in federal parliament E.D. Cash, a Liberal member from Western Australia, asked the Minister for Air, F.M. Osborne, whether his department (specifically Air Force Intelligence) had investigated the reports. The minister's reply did not address this question, but instead focused on the general situation, indicating that most sightings of UFOs were explained and 'that only a very small percentage, something like 3 per cent of reported sightings of flying objects cannot be explained'. A representative of one UFO group was advised by the Directorate of Air Force Intelligence that the Department was awaiting 'depth of evidence' on the New Guinea sightings.

However, the department had not even interviewed Gill. Finally the Minister for Defence requested a report and the RAAF interviewed Gill on 29 December 1959, some six months after the sighting. Gill's recollection of the visit is that the two officers from Canberra talked about stars and planets and then left. He heard no more from them.

As one might expect, Gill's account was dismissed by the RAAF despite its extraordinary nature and the number of witnesses. The senior interviewing officer, Squadron Leader F.A. Lang, concluded:

'Although the Reverend Gill could be regarded as a reliable observer, it is felt that the June/July incidents could have been nothing more than natural phenomena coloured by past events and subconscious influences of UFO enthusiasts. During the period of the report the weather was cloudy and unsettled with light thunder storm. Although it is not possible to draw firm conclusions, an analysis of rough bearings and angles above the horizon does suggest that at least some of the lights observed were the planets Jupiter, Saturn and Mars.

Light refraction, the changing position of the planet relative to the observer and cloud movement would give the impression of size and rapid movement. In addition varying cloud densities could account for the human shapes and their sudden appearance and disappearance'.

My own close analysis of the reports suggests that the RAAF 'explanation' of either known planets seen through fast moving cloud, or natural phenomena' does not bear up.

Over the years there have been a number of 'explanations' put forward to account for the Boianai sightings, including astronomical misidentification, hoax, cargo cult effects, and that Gill had myopia and astigmatism. (In fact at the time he was wearing correctly prescribed glasses). None of these satisfactorily address the evidence. Dr Alien Hynek, and staff at his Centre for UFO Studies, went to great lengths to investigate and research the affair.

Hynek and Alien Hendry, the centre's chief investigator, concluded the 'lesser UFOs' seen by Gill were attributable to bright stars and planets, but not the primary object. Its size and absence of movement over three hours ruled out an astronomical explanation. My own discussions with Gill led me to the same conclusion.

Most recently there was an attempt at explaining the whole affair away by suggesting that Gill and the other witnesses were confused by a false horizon, and that all they had been watching was a brightly lit squidboat and crew too busy to do more than just wave at the people on shore. This idea is not tenable when one realises that Gill was certain that the object he saw was at a 30 degree elevation in the sky. A more radical attempt to dispose of the Gill case came from UFO sceptic Daniel Cohen in his book Myths of the Space Age.

The Boianai visitations are enshrined in a classic piece of Australian fiction. Novelist Randolph Stow's 1979 book "Visitants", which has the Boianai visitations as a backdrop to a striking story of confrontation and disintegration, emerged from Stow's experience as a cadet patrol officer in Papua-New Guinea. He was an assistant to the Government Anthropologist. His novel opens with this sentence: 'On June 26, 1959, at Boianai in Papua, visitants appeared to the Reverend William Booth Gill, himself a visitant of thirteen years standing, and to thirty-seven witnesses of another colour.'

The Boianai 'visitants' still stand as remarkable evidence for an impressive aerial anomaly and are regarded as some of the best entity reports on record. At the time of writing I spoke again with

Gill. He still remains puzzled by what he saw and was pleased that an authority like Dr Hynek had independently interviewed him and some of the other witnesses and travelled to the site. While he accepts that the sightings remain unexplained, he questioned my characterisation of some attempts to explain them as 'silly'. He felt that these 'explanations' were serious attempts to bring understanding to the events. I think that attitude encapsulate the integrity of Gill and the reality of the affair.

In 1973, Alien Hynek visited Australia and Papua New Guinea and found six of the witnesses to the Boianai events. They all supported Gill's version of what had happened.

The Kelly-Hopkinsville 'Goblins' Encounter

Full Report/Article

Kelly is a small town, and Hopkinsville a small city, both located in rural Christian County in southwestern Kentucky. "Lucky" Sutton's family farm was located nearer to Kelly, but the nearest police were in Hopkinsville. Thus, this case acquired the name Kelly-Hopkinsville.

Date August 21, 1955
Location Kelly, Kentucky, United States

At around 7.00 P.M. on August 21, a visiting Pennsylvania man named Billy Ray Taylor went out to fetch some water from the Sutton family well. While he was at the well, he saw a large shining object land in a gully about a city block away. He went back inside and told the others, but they laughed and didn't believe him.

A short time later the family dog began barking wildly outside, so Carl "Lucky" Sutton and Billy Ray grabbed their guns and went out to investigate. They had walked a few yards from the front door when they saw a small 3-to-4 foot creature walking towards them with its hands up, as if surrendering. They later described the creature as having large eyes, a long thin mouth, large ears, thin short legs, and hands ending in claws.

In a rural area in the 1950s, folks were likely to shoot first and ask questions later if they felt threatened. Even though the creature seemed to be peaceful, Billy Ray fired a shot at it with his .22, and Lucky blasted away with his shotgun. They couldn't possibly have missed the creature at that range, but it just did a quick back flip and ran quickly into the woods, apparently unharmed.

Billy Ray and Lucky returned to the house, but before they could tell the others what had happened, the creature, or another one like it, appeared in front of a window. They shot at him through the screen, leaving a hole that investigators noticed later. When the men went outside to see if they had killed the creature, they found nothing. As they looked, one of the creatures, from the roof of the house, reached down to touch one of the men's hair. They shot at it, but it just floated to the ground and then ran off into the woods.

They went back inside and soon the house was under siege by a group of the creatures. The seven adults and four children in the house at the time were terrified as creature after creature appeared at windows around the house, seemingly taunting them. The men's guns were totally ineffective against the creatures.

After about three hours of this, the family decided to make a run for it. They piled into two vehicles and drove down to the local police station to report the event, arriving at about 11:00 P.M.. When police officers were finally persuaded to go to the farm and investigate, they could find no evidence of the strange events except for gunshot holes in the windows and walls.

According to reports, Sheriff Russell Greenwell was among the twenty-five or so law enforcement officers investigating the scene and the family who had told this wild tale. By all accounts, the witnesses were determined to be sane, not drinking, and in such a state of terror that no one who talked to them doubted that they had seen something unusual. Neighbours reported hearing the shooting, and one person had seen "lights in the sky" earlier that evening.

Shortly after the police left, at about 2:15 A.M., the creatures returned. As before, they began staring into windows, curious but not hostile. Again the men responded with gunfire, and again it had no effect. This ordeal continued until a half an hour before sunrise. On the morning of the 22nd, the police, along with the Air Force, investigated but again found nothing. Billy Ray and Lucky weren't there, having driven to Evansville, Indiana to take care of some sort of business. The Hopkinsville newspaper, The Kentucky New Era, carried the story on 8/22/55.

Many people believe this case to be a complete hoax. If it was then it has to be one of the biggest and most useless hoaxes in ufology to date. The family made no money from the incident and did not want any publicity at the time. They had to make extensive repairs to the house which cost them a considerable sum of money for that year. In the course of shooting at the creatures, Billy Ray and Lucky had shot up the house pretty well. All seven adults told the same story with no contradictory evidence in their statements. Sketches of the creatures based on descriptions from different witnesses matched closely. Their stories were unwavering a year later when a thorough investigation of the case was conducted by Isabel Davis.

No evidence of a hoax has ever been revealed in this case, and the Suttons still insisted that it was true years later. Now, over forty years later, it's likely that many, if not all, of the Suttons who were adults at the time have gone to their graves without changing their story.

Noted astronomer and ufologist J. Allen Hynek took the story seriously because he discussed the case with two of the principal investigators of the story: Bud Ledwith, an engineer at a radio station in Hopkinsville and a personal acquaintance of Hynek's, and Isabel Davis, an investigator from New York City.

The Flatwoods Monster

Full Report/Article

On September 12, 1952, a small group of boys spotted a pulsating, reddish sphere float around a hill, hover briefly and then drop behind the crest of another in the small town of Flatwoods, West Virginia (population 300). From the far side of the hill a bright glow shone, as if from a landed object. On their way to see what had landed the boys were joined by others that had witnessed the flying spectacle, including beautician Kathleen May, her two sons and their friend Tommy Hyer, seventeen-year-old Eugeen Lemon

Date September 12, 1952
Location Flatwoods, West Virginia, United States

and his dog. The dog ran ahead of the group and was briefly out of sight as it ran around the hill. Suddenly it was heard barking furiously and then came running back, fleeing with its tail between its legs, apparently in fear. A foul smelling mist covered the ground making the searchers eyes water. The two leading the group, Lemon and Neil Nunley, got to the top of the hill first and observed a "big ball of fire" fifty feet to their right. Others in the group said it was the size of a house.

To the groups left, on the hilltop just under the branches of a large oak tree, were two small, blue lights. At Mrs. May's suggestion, Lemon pointed his flashlight in their direction. To everybody's horror, the flashlight highlighted a grotesque looking creature with a head shaped like the "ace of spades," as several of the witnesses independently described it. Inside the head was a circular "window," dark except for the two lights from which pale blue beams extended straight ahead. In their quick observation of the being, they could see nothing that resembled arms or legs. The creature, which seemed to be over six feet tall, moved towards the witnesses. It seemed to be gliding rather than walking. Seconds later, it changed direction and began heading for the glowing sphere from which it apparently had come from.

All of this took place in the matter of a few moments, during which time Lemon fainted. The others dragged him with them as they ran from the scene. When interviewed about a half an hour later, by A. Lee Stewart Jr., a reporter for the Braxton Democrat, the witnesses were barely able to speak. Some sought first aid. Stewart felt that there was no question that they had seen something that had badly frightened them. Soon afterwards, after Lemon had recovered, Stewart and Lemon went to the spot where they had seen the creature and the strange craft. Stewart also noted that there was an acrid odour in the air that irritated his nose and throat. He returned alone to the site first thing the next morning. He found "skid marks" going down the hill towards a large area of recently matted grass, which seemed to indicated that a large object had rested there.

The encounter, which the newspapers quickly dubbed "The Flatwoods Monster" sighting. It took place during a flurry of sightings of unusual flying objects in the region. Bailey Frame, a resident of nearby Birch River, reported seeing a bright orange ball circling over the area where the monster was spotted. It was visible for around fifteen minutes before veering off towards the airport at Sutton, where the object was also reported. According to an account, one week before the Flatwoods event, a Weston woman and her mother encountered the same or similar creature. The younger woman was so frightened that she needed hospitilization after the event. Both also reported the noxious odour.

Years later, writer John Keel interviewed a couple who claimed that on the evening following the original sighting, and ten to fifteen miles to the southwest of it, they encountered a ten foot tall creature emitting a foul odour. It approached their stalled car then returned to the woods. Moments later, a luminous, pulsating sphere arose from the trees and ascended into the sky.

Many skeptics have claimed that what May and her companions had seen a meteor and an owl, and had mistaken these for the strange things that they reported. Nonetheless, when interviewed shortly after the incident, the witnesses told a story that investigators found strikingly consistent. When interviewed in the early part of the 1990's, Kathleen May Horner recalled that two men, first identifying themselves as reporters, then acknowledging they were employees of the government, interviewed her. This is not hard to believe; it is a fact that the U.S. Air Force dispatched two plainclothes investigators to the scene. Like the skeptics, they laid the incident down to hysteria inflamed by an owl and a meteor.

Man Encounters Humanoids at Varese, Italy (The Bruno Facchini Case)

Full Report/Article

On April 24, 1950, at a place called Abbiate Guaz-zone (Varese region — 45D 49 N., 8° 50 E.), which lies slightly to the east of Lake Maggiore in Northern Italy, the 42-year-old worker Bruno Facchini was the protagonist of a truly mind-boggling experience which, at the time, received widespread treatment both in the Italian regular press and in the "Rivista Aeronautica" (Aeronautical Review).

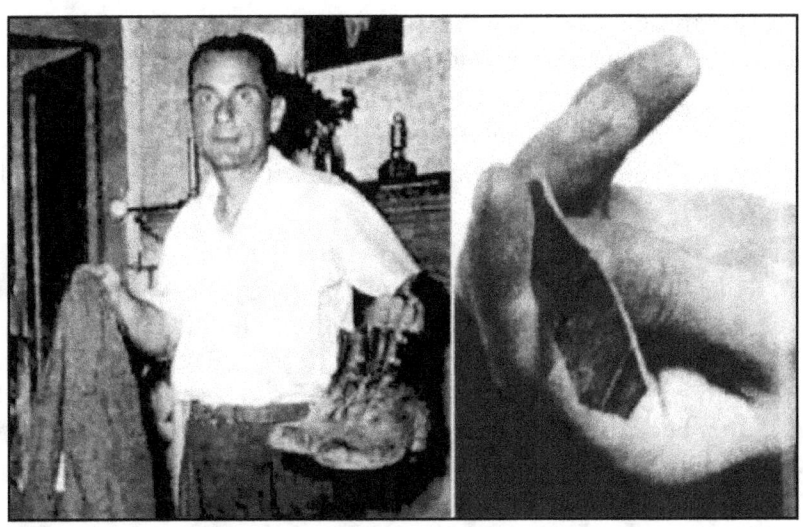

Date April 24, 1950
Location Varese, Italy

Facchini, a capable and highly esteemed worker, employed at the time in a local firm, was living in a little house on the outskirts of the village. He had stepped outside from the house [and noticed a flash.] [When he went to investigate], he perceived an enormous black shadow, almost round, "like a ball flattened from above". In the middle of it there was a small ladder, from the top of which was coming a faint greenish light, and he was now able to see at close hand the source of the flashing. An individual wearing a "diver's suit" and a mask, on top of a sort of pneumatic lift, seemed to be welding something. The hull of the craft, lit by the glow from the welding, gave off metallic reflections. Two other individuals, about 1.70 m in height, also in "divers' suits", were moving very slowly around the craft, as though hampered by the suits they were wearing. Over their faces they wore masks of the same dark colour as the "divers' suits", terminating at the level of the mouth in a tube with a little opening at the end.

Facchini's first thought was that it was a military aircraft in difficulty (the military airfields of Vergiate and Venegono were only a few kilometers distant), and he went up and asked if he could be of any help. The response was some incomprehensible guttural sounds. Meanwhile, in the interior of the object, he had caught sight of a second ladder, and all around on the walls, tubes, cylinders, and gauges. At the same time, he noticed a noise "like the sound of a gigantic beehive".

At that point it was that Bruno Facchini grasped that he was in the presence of no aeroplane. Seized with panic, he took to his heels.

Turning back as he ran, he saw one of the crew point at him a sort of "photographic apparatus" that he was wearing round his neck, and shoot a beam of light at him. He felt immediately as though he had been struck by a powerful jet of compressed air and it sent him rolling on the ground. Bruised and aching, but perfectly conscious, Facchini then saw the lift descend, bringing down with it the individual with the welding equipment, and then reduce in size until it (the lift) was a sort of small box. Then the crew put it into the craft. The ladder was now drawn in and the door closed. Then the hum that Facchini had heard right at the start became louder and, a few instants later, the craft rose and vanished at a fantastic speed into the darkness of the night.

Next day, Facchini reported the matter to the Police Station in Varese, and the Authorities started their investigations at the spot. On the ground, which was quite hard, were visible four round impressions about one meter in diameter and distant about six meters from each other and set in a square. The grass was scorched or withered, and some small fragments of metal were found at the site; probably the remains from the welding. They were of a shiny metal with a granulous surface which, when analyzed, was defined as "an anti-friction metal", very resistant to heat.

With a view to completing the investigative picture, the journalist Renato Vesco subsequently had an analysis made of a few metal fragments from a piece that Facchini had kept...

[The conclusion was that the fragments] are... of a "lead bronze", with a high content of tin...

The Villa Santina Case (Two Humanoids Encountered by Italian Artist)

Full Report/Article

On June 24, 1947, Airman Kenneth Arnold startled the world with his claim to have seen nine discshaped objects travelling in line ahead, and at fantastic speed, through the skies over Mount Rainier. Arnold likened the objects, and their movements, to "saucers skimming over water". The era of the flying saucer was upon us.

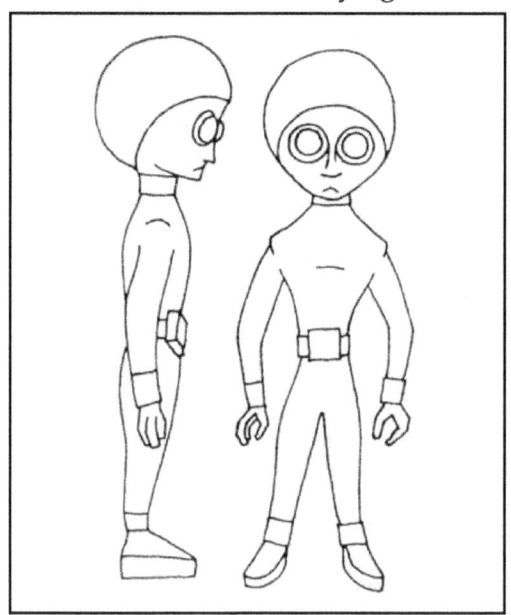

Date August 14, 1947
Location Villa Santina, Italy

Seven weeks later, according to Italian artist R. L. Johannis, there took place what was probably the first post-Arnold "landing with entities" case in Europe. The story has been recorded in the May 1964 edition of Clypeus (organ of Centra Studi Clipeologici of Turin), and by Antonio Ribera in his book El Gran Enigma de los Platillos Volanies.

Signor Johannis was out painting near the Chiarso creek, at Villa Santina, close by Carnia (Friuli), on August 14, 1947. The time was about 9 A.M. Suddenly he noticed a 30 ft. disc-shaped object that had alighted some little distance from him. Next, Signor Johannis saw two child-sized beings standing alongside the object. The artist said that they were about 3 feet tall, and were wearing dark blue coveralls with a bright red collar and belt. They also wore spherical helmets on heads that seemed larger than normal, but their faces were not covered. Their faces had a greenish colour, their eyes were large and plum coloured with a vertical line (the pupil?) in the centre, and they had no eyelashes or eyebrows. Each had a straight and rather large nose. Their hands were claw-like, greenish in colour, and with eight fingers on each, four opposed to four in the same way that our thumbs are opposed to our fingers.

With his paint brushes still in his hand, the artist hailed the creatures. It is possible that this was interpreted as a hostile gesture, for one of the beings touched the centre of its belt and projected a thin vapour which caused the artist to fall dazed onto his back. The creatures then approached to within two yards of the prostrate artist and stood examining his easel. Although weak, the artist contrived to roll over, and saw the beings pick up the easel which had been knocked down; he perceived that it was taller than both of them. He also noticed that they were panting heavily. They then returned to the disc-shaped object and entered it, whereupon it rose from the ground, hovered and, according to the account, disappeared.

When the unfortunate artist had sufficiently recovered his strength to be able to stand, he saw that his easel had disappeared.

Alien Abductions

Since the term 'flying saucer' was first coined in 1947, a staggering 40 million unidentified flying object (UFO) sightings have been logged. One in ten Americans claims to have had some sort of encounter with an alien. Over 30 UFO crash landings have been reported and abduction reports run into the tens of thousands.

Now many of these people could be deluded…….or, indeed, lying, but many of them truly believe that they are telling the truth. While some abductees have made a fortune from books and films about their experiences, others have shied away from publicity, not wanting people to think that they were cranks or just plain crazy. Some abductees have been policemen and ministers of the cloth, whose reputation and livelihoods were at stake, but they still spoke out.

True, few people have a clear recollection of being abducted; most claim that they discovered that they had been abducted when they realized that they were 'missing time'. This phenomenon occurs when an abductee has seen a UFO and then finds that they have no memory of the following period. UFO investigators use a technique called regressive hypnosis to try to uncover what happened during that missing time, in which the hypnotist puts the abductee into a trance and takes them back to relive their experiences. Sometimes the victim is so terrified by what happened that they blank it from their minds, even when they are in the deepest trance, Others recall 'false memories', which were either implanted by the aliens to cover their tracks or were evoked by the abductee to hide the awful truth from themselves. But by delicate probing the hypnotist can often reveal the details of the abduction ordeal.

Some victims are abducted just once, others many times throughout their lives. Some are constantly plagued by aliens invading their homes at night. Whole families can be abducted separately, or together. There are several types of aliens involved.

In the USA, most aliens these days are short – usually about 4 foot 6 inches (1.37 m) – and look like a foetus. They have no hair, vestigial eyes and ears and huge, black, pupil-less eyes. They also have long, thin arms and three or four tapering fingers, like the eponymous ET's (extraterrestrial's). They are ugly and rarely have genitals. These forms of alien are known as 'greys', because of their grey skins.

Americans used to see aliens that were of the 'Nordic' type. They are tall and good-looking, with blond hair and blue eyes – the type that is common in Europe nowadays; however, greys seem to have been creeping into Britain recently. Nordics nearly always wear the Bacofoil suits that were so popular in 1950s' sci-fi movies. They sometimes appear with greys, but more often use small robots to carry out menial tasks for them. In South America, aliens come in a bizarre range of types. Many are hairy.

It is difficult to explain why differing types of alien should visit different continents, although some abductees say that they have been told that there is competition between the various species of alien. Experts explain that aliens are so beyond our comprehension that they manifest themselves in the various ways that different cultures have learned to understand. That is why, as human culture becomes more globalised, abductees' descriptions have become more consistent, the experts say.

Alien abductions occur in different ways, too. Some people are lured-perhaps subliminally – to deserted spots from which they can be abducted. They may then be marched up a ramp or a ladder on to the aliens' spacecraft. Sometimes the aliens come to an abductee's bedside, even while their partner is sleeping beside them, before paralyzing their victim and floating them out of the bedroom window. On other occasions a car, along with all of its passengers, is beamed on board by a column of light.

Once aboard, abductees go through a range of experiences. Some are taken to distant planets, while some are given a whistle-stop tour of the Earth by creatures who say that they live on the planet but don't get out much. Others are shown films depicting the destruction of the Earth, or another planet, and are warned of the dangers of war and pollution. Yet others are seized for medical experimentation or sexual purposes.

Strangely enough, most of the good-looking, female aliens head for South America, from which they abduct Latin lovers for a night of passion on their spacecraft. In North America and Britain it is the male aliens who grab human women and then seduce or rape them. The aliens often complain that their race cannot reproduce and explain that they are trying to create hybrid babies with earthlings. As a result, lots of female abductees say that they have been put through unpleasant gynaecological examinations. This is the commonest element in the abduction stories told by female abductees, who sometimes believe that their eggs have been taken. And such women also often report having implants inserted up their noses or into incisions made in their legs.

Some women find that they have been impregnated by aliens, but then mysteriously lose the body, often after a second abduction. (It is thought that the aliens take the developing foetus and incubate it elsewhere). Women sometimes report seeing what they believe is their hybrid offspring during later abductions.

Aliens are interested in the male genitalia, too: men recall having been fitted with suction devices and then having had their semen extracted. This, apparently, is all part of the aliens' hideous genetic experiment.

You may find some of the stories in this book. Others may sound like sexual fantasies – or sexual anxieties – that have been projected into outer space. Even so, they still represent the world's greatest alien – abduction stories. Some are hard to shake off. You may be able to identify which ones are drug-induced, or half-remembered dreams, delusions, the result of lack of sleep or motorway hypnosis, or those which are plain rubbish – it is difficult to say where the line should be drawn. But many of the stories presented here have a bizarre consistency that is not easily explained away; something is happening out there. So once you have discarded the stories that you find too incredible to be true, what you have left will undoubtedly constitute the world's greatest alien abductions case files.

Villas Boas Case

Full Report/Article
Date: 22 February 1958
Subject: Antonio Villas Boas.
Location: Surgery of Dr Olavo Fontes, Rio De Janeiro.
Statement Witnesses: Dr Olavo Fontes, Joao Martins (journalist).

Date October 14, 1957
Location Sao Francisco de Sales, Central Brazil

"My name is Antonio Villas Boas, I am twenty three years old and a farmer by profession. I live with my family on a farm which belongs to us. It is situated near the town of Sao Francisco de Sales in the state of Minas Gerais, near the border of the state of Sao Paulo. I have two brothers and three sisters, who all live in the neighbourhood; another brother and sister are dead. All the male members of the family work on the farm. There are many fields and plantations which must be cultivated. We have a petrol driven tractor which we use in two shifts when the fields have to be tilled. The farm workers we employ work during the day. At night I plough mostly alone or with one of my brothers. I am unmarried and in good health, I work hard and am taking a correspondence course and study as often as I can. It was a sacrifice to come to Rio, as I am urgently needed on the farm. But I thought it my duty to report on the unusual events in which I was involved. I will do everything which you think right – and I am also ready to make a declaration to the civil or military authorities."

So Antonio Villas Boas began to recount one of the most incredible yet fascinating abduction cases in the history of the UFO phenomenon.

1. The First Sightings

The sightings first started on the night of October 5 1957. Antonio was resting in his bedroom (his brother Joao was resting there also) when, as a result of the stifling heat in the room, Antonio opened the bedroom shutters. When he looked out into the farmyard a strange sight greeted his eyes – a large area of the farmyard was bathed in a brilliant light. When Antonio couldn't see where the source of his light was situated he tried to rouse his brother but the latter merely told Antonio to try and get some rest and ignore it. Antonio closed the shutters.

But his curiousity got the better of him and made it impossible for him to sleep. He opened the shutters once more and noticed that the blinding light still shone in the yard. Suddenly it moved on to the window and Antonio snapped the shutters closed in alarm. The noise awakened the slumbering Joao and they both watched the light as it streamed through the shutters. The light then moved up and over the roof, gleaming through the tiles. (Due to the hot climate there were no false ceilings in the farnmhouse). After a few unnerving moments the light disappeared and didn't return.

On October 14, at around 9:30pm, Antonio Villas Boas and one of his brothers were out working in one of the fields when they became aware of a bright red light hovering over the northern end of the field.

Antonio decided to investigate the phenomenon and asked his brother to accompany him, the latter declined but Antonio was intrigued and decided to carry on alone. As he neared the hovering light it suddenly sped away to the other end of the field. Once more Antonio followed the mysterious light and to be met by the same behaviour, the light simply sped away in the opposite direction. This happened several times and eventually Antonio gave up the chase and returned to where his brother was working. The light disappeared soon after.

2. Abduction

The following night Antonio was ploughing alone in the same field. A strange red light mysteriously appeared in the sky, increasing in size as it came nearer. In a matter of a few seconds a shining egg shaped object was hovering about 160 feet above the Brazilian farmer.

The object sank to the ground, using three long spikes near its base to land roughly about 40 feet in front of Antonio's tractor. Distressed, Antonio jumped onto the tractor and tried to drive away but several seconds later the engine and the headlights cut out. The only light now was coming from the object itself, which emitted a strange red glow.

Antonio tried to frantically restart the tractor when suddenly someone grabbed his arm. Antonio pushed the small, helmeted figure backwards and tried to make a run for it. However, several other entities grabbed him and dragged the struggling farmer into the object. As they dragged him away his shouting caused the entities to stop and observe him, this happened every time he opened his mouth.

Taken up a small ramp and ladder into the craft Antonio was lowered to the floor. They were in a small square shaped room, the door to the outside now closed behind them.

There appeared to be around five entities altogether standing around watching him, eventually one of the small beings ushered Antonio into another room. This room was brightly lit like the last but was larger in size and oval shaped, Boas later believed that this must have been the centre of the craft. In the middle of this room stood a round pillar that narrowed in the middle and the only other furnishings were an unusually shaped table and several round bar type stools.

The other entities gathered around him and communicated in what seemed like a succession of animal like grunts. Boas recalled this language as being unlike anything he had ever heard before and bore no resemblance whatsoever to human speech. Boas also noticed that they all wore the same tight fitting grey overalls, which looked almost like wetsuits. He couldn't see their faces properly because a large helmet obscured them, only the piercing glass blue eyes were visible.

3. Tests

The entities began to undress the farmer and when he was completely naked one of the beings rubbed a thick yet odourless fluid over his bare skin. This fluid made Villas Boas feel even colder (it was apparently much colder inside the craft anyway) but as the fluid dried the freezing sensation died away. After this he was led into another smaller chamber.

A few moments passed when two of the entities brought some odd looking equipment into the room. This equipment was then used to collect a blood sample from two wounds inflicted on Boas's chin. After this sample was taken, the entities left.

Time passed and the cold and frightened captive began to sense a rather sickening smell. Several small holes on one of the walls were introducing a thick, pungent smoke into the room. He became extremely ill, but after he had vomited in the corner of the room the air mysteriously cleared.

Some time later the door opened and a small naked woman walked in. Her hair was blonde and she had large almond shaped eyes. She had exceptionally high cheekbones which gave the impression of a rather pointed chin. Boas also noted that the woman's pubic hair appeared to be red in colour but apart from these features the farmer maintained that she looked relatively normal.

When the door closed the woman approached him and began to rub her face against his body. Villas Boas reckoned that the fluid smeared on him earlier may have had something to do with this. With her actions Boas became very excited and responded to her. Antonio claimed that it was a 'normal' act, spoiled only by her habit of growling and snarling. After their second bout of interplanetary relations the spacewoman preserved a sample of Boas's sperm in a small container before leaving the room. As she departed she made a quick symbolic gesture –pointing first at herself, then at Antonio then pointing upwards.

As she left one of the beings returned with Antonio's clothing. Dressing quickly he moved out of the small bare chamber and back into the room with the central column.

Antonio tried to steal a piece of equipment that resembled a clock from the table around which some of the entities were sitting. However, he was spotted doing this and one of the beings angrily wrenched it back. At that point Boas decided to behave himself.

4. Leaving The Craft

One of the entities signalled Antonio to follow him. They both moved into the first room and Antonio noticed that the door to the outside was open. They moved through a doorway and clambered onto a small metal pathway that was attached to the side of the ship. They both walked around the strange craft, the entity pointing out various things on the way probably linked to the ships means of propulsion.

Eventually the being indicated for Antonio to leave so Boas quickly staggered down the ramp and onto the freshly ploughed field. He turned around to watch the craft and the entity gestured to him, exactly as the naked woman had – pointing at himself, then Antonio then upwards at the stars. The being moved inside the door which closed immediately behind him.

Antonio Villas Boas watched as the craft ascended in a blaze of light and shot away at a tremendous speed. Wearily, he moved back to where he had left the tractor and noticed that it was now 5:30 A.M. Boas had been in the craft for around four and a half hours.

5. After The Event

While Boas only spoke of his encounter to his family and a handful of friends the rumours eventually found their way to two of Brazils more prominent UFO researchers, Dr. Olavo Fontes and the journalist Joao Martins. Alongside the physical complications, the psychological damage was understandably huge and Villas Boas was unable to return to normal day to day living for some time. Medical tests conducted by Dr Olavo Fontes appeared to indicate that Boas had indeed experienced something very strange. Fontes concluded that many of the symptoms shown by Boas over the months after the event were a direct result of exposure to radiation.

The Brazilian Secret Service hushed the case up as at that time there was a huge flap of UFO sightings in the country. Had this case been leaked to the press it was feared that it would have resulted in widespread panic. Indeed, it wasn't until 1980 that Villas Boas commented in public on his strange, unnerving but fascinating encounter. He never accepted any money to capitalise on the sensational aspects of the story, nor did he ever consider selling the whole thing when the enforced silence was over. Boas always wanted to forget the whole incident and get on with his life.

Boas continued his studies and pursued a career in law, eventually becoming an attorney in Formosa.

He passed away in 1992 and in his lifetime never withdrew his claims.

Betty and Barney Hill Case

Full Report/Article

New Hampshire is a marvelous and mysterious place. In the southern part of the state is North Salem, near which lies Mystery Hill, "America's Stonehenge", a collection of stone structures with a mysterious origin. Also in the south, near New Hampshire's small strip of coastline, is Exeter, the site of a large number of UFO sightings in 1965.

Date September 19, 1961
Location Exeter, New Hampshire, United States

In the eastern central part of the state is Ossipee Lake, an area sacred to the Indians. In 1800, an Indian burial ground was discovered in the area that contained over ten thousand bodies arranged in concentric circles. There are numerous "kettle" lakes in the area that were carved out by glaciers during the ice ages, and the area is ringed by ancient volcanoes. Some of the ponds are considered bottomless and may be connected to each other by volcanic vents. It is said that UFOs have been seen plunging into these deep ponds.

Further north and in the centre of New Hampshire lies the White Mountains National Forest. In the summer, the area is filled with vacationers and campers and hikers and fishermen. There are various sights to see, such as the Flume, The Old Man of the Mountain, Mount Washington, and Indian Head. In the winter, skiers flock to the slopes and hunters to the forests. But during the in-between times, the early fall and the early spring, the area is quiet, resting.

It probably wasn't easy having a mixed marriage in 1961, even in liberal New Hampshire, but the Hills seemed to have adjusted well. Betty Hill was a white social worker, and Barney Hill was a black postal employee. Barney was working in Boston, commuting back and forth daily from Portsmouth, New Hampshire, where the couple lived. Barney had developed an ulcer, perhaps from stress at work, and when the opportunity came for a few days' vacation, he took it. Betty was able to schedule her vacation for the same time, so they decided to go to Canada. They took their little dachsund, Delsey, with them, staying in motels that would allow the dog in their room.

They went to Niagara Falls and to Montreal, and on September 19th, they were on their way back home to Portsmouth. They stopped in Colebrook for a burger and then wound on down Highway 3 through Lancaster.

At about 10:15PM, just south of Lancaster, Barney noticed a light in the sky below the moon, and called Betty's attention to it. At first they thought it was a planet, but then they noticed it was moving. Barney began trying to convince himself that it was only a satellite or a plane, becoming more and more agitated at anything that contradicted this view. Betty, whose sister had seen a UFO, was convinced from the start that the light in the sky was something unusual. They stopped the car to let Delsey do her business, and observed the object with a pair of binoculars they had.

By the time they reached the Flume, north of North Woodstock, the object had grown in size and Barney noticed that it had an unusual motion in that it would dart away to the west and then back, closer each time. At Indian Head, Barney stopped the car again and looked at the object with the binoculars. He could now see multi-colored lights and rows of windows on the pancake-shaped object, which was huge and was only a hundred feet away. He walked closer to the craft, and could see occupants standing inside, one of which he said seemed to be the "leader". He became very frightened and ran back to the car, where Betty was waiting. He started the car and took off quickly. They could no longer see the object, but they heard a beeping noise.

Sometime later, they heard the beeping noise again, and noticed that they were thirty-five miles south of Indian Head, at Ashland. They drove on home to Portsmouth without further incident.

They slept until afternoon, and when they awoke, Betty called her sister Janet and told her about their experience. Janet urged her to report the UFO sighting to nearby Pease Air Force Base. Over Barney's objections, Betty called the base and gave a report to Major Paul W. Henderson of the 100th Bomb Wing. When asked to do so by the Major, Barney reluctantly gave his version of the sighting. Curiously, Pease AFB was the home of the 509th Bomb Wing in 1961, the same 509th Bomb Wing whose home had been Roswell AAFB at the time of the "Roswell Incident" in 1947. According to Jacques Vallee in Dimensions, the Hills' sighting was corroborated by a radar sighting at Pease AFB on 20 September 1961, but his reference for this is unclear. It's an excerpt from Report No. 100-1-61, that says simply:

...a strange incident occurred at 0214 local on 20 Sept. No importance was attached to the incident at the time.

Aftermat

After reporting the incident, Barney preferred to forget about the event, but Betty went to the library to look up books on UFOs. She found Major Donald Kehoe's The Flying Saucer Conspiracy and read it avidly. She even wrote Kehoe a letter detailing their sighting.

A few days later, ten days after their sighting, Betty began to have a series of nightmares that lasted five days and then stopped. The nightmares involved she and Barney being stopped at a road block and then being taken inside some large craft. At the urging of a friend, Betty wrote down the dreams.

Meanwhile, Betty's letter to Kehoe had been passed to Walter Webb, a lecturer on the staff of the Hayden Planetarium in Boston. Webb was a scientific advisor for NICAP (National Investigations Committee on Aerial Phenomenon), Kehoe's UFO organization. Webb was asked to interview the Hills. He drove up to Portsmouth and spent several hours interviewing them. He was much impressed with their sincerity and with the detail they provided, and he wrote a long report for NICAP.

After talking to Keyhoe, and after reading Webb's report, two technical writers who were interested in UFOs, Robert Hohman and C.D. Jackson, made arrangements to interview the Hills in November. It was during this interview that one of the writers asked a key question: Why had it taken the Hills so long to get home? Calculating the time and the mileage from Colebrook to Portsmouth showed that they should have gotten home two hours sooner than they did, even allowing for stops. Also present at this interview was Major James MacDonald, a former Air Force Intelligence officer and close friend of the Hills. It was he who first suggested hypnosis to recover their memory of the missing time period.

In March of 1962, they spoke to a psychiatrist about hypnosis, but decided to put it off until a later date. That summer, Barney's ulcers returned, and his recurring hypertention returned. Feeling that his problems were emotional in origin, he began therapy with a psychiatrist in Exeter, Dr. Stephens. He continued this therapy through the next year, but the UFO sighting was not explored as part of this treatment at first. But, not long after Betty and Barney had been asked to speak to a church group about their sighting, Dr. Stephens decided that the sighting was important. He also decided that hypnosis was needed to help Barney deal with the incident. Not being proficient in hypnosis himself, he referred Barney to Dr. Benjamin Simon, a well-known Boston psychiatrist and neurologist.

Dr. Simon quickly determined that he should treat both Betty and Barney for an anxiety syndrome that could be traced back to the incident on the night of September 19-20, 1961. He began by hypnotizing Barney, then Betty. Over the next six months, the story of the two hours of missing time began to emerge. Betty and Barney Hill told of being stopped at a roadblock and being taken onto the UFO, where they were given medical examinations before being returned to their car. Betty reported being shown a "star map" that was later interpreted to mean that the aliens came from Zeta Reticuli. Their story was later written into a two-part article in Look magazine, a book titled The Interrupted Journey by John G. Fuller, and later a TV movie called The UFO Incident starring Estelle Parsons and James Earl Jones as the Hills.

The Hill's story was the first "modern" abduction story. There was no Communion back in 1961, and no X-Files. Abduction stories had not become part of the popular culture yet. People had claimed to have contact with aliens, but they were "contactees" in the mold of George Adamski, who claimed to have been visited by friendly Venusians with long blond hair who gave him a warning for all mankind about nuclear war. Skeptics such as Martin S. Kottmeyer claim that the elements of the Hill abduction could be found in movies like 1953's Invaders From Mars and in the pulp science fiction magazines. They also say that an alien with wrap-around eyes such as Barney Hill described was portrayed on an episode of Outer Limits just 12 days before the hypnotic session during which he described the aliens. These claims might be compelling if it had ever been proven that Betty and Barney had seen the movie or the Outer Limits episode or that they were science fiction fans. But investigators such as Karl Pflock say that there is no evidence that they had been exposed to any of those things. Skeptics also point out that Betty's nightmares began after she read Keyhoe's book. That's true, but Barney had not read Kehoe's book when he saw the UFO with double rows of windows with "people" behind them on the night of the sighting.

Even if the dreams and the hypnotically recalled "abduction" are excluded for whatever reason, the sighting itself still stands as one of the most reliable and inexplicable on record.

Dr. Simon, the psychiatrist who worked through the post-traumatic stress of the incident with the Hills, did not believe that they were lying. He was unable to explain the sighting as anything other than an actual occurrence, and stated as much in a letter to the insurance company regarding the case. However, he did not believe that the abduction took place. His final diagnosis was that Betty's mind had created dreams of an abduction to fill the amnesia period, and that Barney's mind, when he heard the content of her dreams, had unconsciously absorbed her dreams for the same purpose of filling the missing time period. None of this, of course, explains exactly what DID happen and why it took the Hills two hours longer than normal to drive from Colebrook to Ashland.

The Betty Andreasson Encounter

Full Report/Article

In the city of South Ashburnham, Massachusetts on the night of January 25 1967, one of the most celebrated cases of UFO abduction began. Betty Andreasson was working in her kitchen while her seven children, mother, and father were in the living room. Shortly after 6:30, the lights in the house briefly blinked. Immediately thereafter, a reddish light began to beam through the kitchen window. The sudden darkness in the house set the kids nerves on edge, and Betty ran to comfort them. Her father ran into the kitchen to peer out the window, and find the source of the unusual light. To his utter shock, he saw five odd-looking beings coming toward the house with a hopping motion!

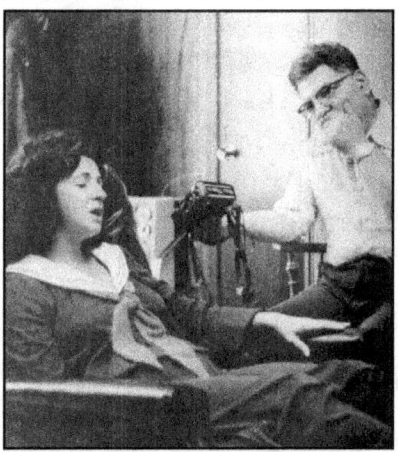

Date January 25, 1967
Location South Ashburnham, Massachusetts, United States

Before he could regain his composure, he saw the beings walk right through the wooden door! What happened next would test the imagination and strength of even an open-minded, adventurous person. The entire family was suddenly put into a state of suspended animation. One of the creatures went to Betty's father, while one of the other four began to make telepathic communication with Betty. One of the group seemed to be a leader of sorts. He was about five-feet tall. The other four appeared to be about a foot shorter. All of the beings had a pear-shaped head, with wide eyes, and small ears and noses. Their mouths were only slits, and never moved, though they were able to communicate through their minds.

The beings wore a type of coverall, blue in color, with a wide belt. There also was a logo of a bird on their sleeves. The hands only had three fingers, and they wore boots. The creatures did not move as a human, but floated as they went. Betty would later relate that, though she was frightened, she felt a sense of calm, even friendship toward the beings. The aliens were holding Betty's children in a frozen state of consciousness, but when Betty showed concern for them, the aliens released her 11-year-old daughter, to assure her the children were not being harmed.

Betty was taken by the aliens outside to a waiting craft which rested on the side of a sloping back yard. The craft was estimated to be about 20 feet in diameter, in the classic UFO shape. Betty believes that after she aboard the craft, it joined a "mother" craft, where she was underwent a physical examination, and also was subjected to the effects of strange equipment. After this, she was given a type of bizarre test, which caused her pain at first, but resulted in a kind of religious experience. Approximately four hours later, she was returned to her home by two of her captors. When she arrived, her entire family was still in a state of suspended animation. One of the beings stayed in her house, evidently to watch the other family members. After releasing the family from the trancelike state, the aliens left.

Betty would later state that the aliens had hypnotized her to not recall any of her experience until a designated time to be determined later. She was able to recall only certain things at the time of her experience; the power outage, the red light through the kitchen window, and the aliens entering the house. Before this bizarre happening, Betty had little or no knowledge of UFO folklore, and being a devoted Christian, she believed that the abduction had a religious meaning. It would be later until she began to view the abduction as alien in nature. Eight years later Betty answered an ad from Dr. J. Allen Hynek, who was soliciting abduction experiences from the general public. Her letter was dismissed at the time, because of it's unusual details, and it would be January 1977, before her story would be fully investigated.

The investigative team assigned to the Andreasson case included a solar physicist, and electronics engineer, an aerospace engineer, a telecommunications specialist, and a UFO investigator. The service of a hypnotist, and a medical doctor trained in psychiatry were also used. Betty's case involved twelve months of investigation. She was given a character-reference check, two lie-detector tests, a psychiatric review, and an excruciating fourteen sessions of regressive hypnosis. The results of this inquiry were startling. Betty, along with her daughter, relived a detailed account of a UFO experience, agreeing on all basic aspects. The results were published in a 528 page account, which stated that Betty and her daughter were sane individuals, who sincerely believe all of the details given in their statements. The Betty Andreasson abduction case is still unsolved to this day.

Police Patrolman Herbert Schirmer Abduction

Full Report/Article

December 3, 1967
2:00 A.M.

Police Patrolman Herbert Schirmer, age 22, was making his rounds. He checked the Ashland Sales Barn, where he found the cattle in an agitated state. He could also hear dogs howling when he got out of his car. Please continue reading below...

Date December 3, 1967
Location Ashland, Nebraska, United States

Finding nothing, he continued his rounds, checking a couple of gas stations along Highway 6.

2:30 A.M.

As Patrolman Schirmer passed through the intersection of Highway 6 with Highway 63 on the outskirts of Ashland, he saw what appeared to be red lights on a large truck stopped a short way down Highway 63. He decided to turn around and check it out. He drove the short distance down 63 and stopped with his headlights shining on the object.

According to Schirmer, the object was definitely not a truck. The red lights that he had seen were blinking through the oval portholes of a metallic, oval-shaped object that was hovering at a height of six to eight feet above the road surface. The object appeared to have a polish aluminum surface and had a sort of catwalk aound it. It had some sort of tripod leg-like structure underneath.

As he watched, the object rose into the air with a sort of siren-like sound and flames coming from underneath it. It passed almost directly over Schirmer's patrol car, then quickly shot out of sight. Schirmer returned to the police station, noting that it was now 3:00 A.M., which surprised him because he felt that only ten minutes had passed. At the station, he made this entry into his logbook: "Saw a flying saucer at the junction of highways 6 and 63. Believe it or not!"

Afterward, Schirmer developed a red welt on his neck, a headache, and he began to feel ill. Word of Schirmer's sighting got to the Condon Commission at the University of Colorado, which was in the process of investigating all available UFO data. Schirmer was asked to come to Boulder, Colorado, which he did. At Boulder, on February 13, 1968, he was hypnotized by psychologist Dr. Leo Sprinkle of the University of Wyoming.

What Hypnosis Revealed

Under hypnosis, Schirmer recalled that, after he stopped his car near the object, the engine died and his radio went silent. A blurred white object came out of the craft and seemed to communicate mentally with him, preventing him from drawing his gun as he intended. After the hypnotic session had ended, Schirmer was able to recall even more details about the encounter. The beings were friendly, they drew energy from electrical power lines, and they had a base on Venus.

The Condon Committee concluded that: "Evaluation of psychological assessment tests, the lack of any evidence, and interviews with the patrolman, left project staff with no confidence that the trooper's reported UFO experience was physically real."

Psychologist Dr. Sprinkle, however, felt that Schirmer "believed in the reality of the events he described."

Returning to Ashland, Schirmer was appointed Ashland's Police Chief when Chief Wlaskin resigned. However, he resigned after two months, unable to concentrate on the job due to his UFO experience. According to Schirmer, he was burned in effigy by some of the townspeople, his car was dynamited, and his wife left him.

Sprinkle's hypnotic sessions with Schirmer barely scratched the surface. Further regression hypnosis sessions were conducted on June 8, 1968 by hypnotist Loring G. Williams and the results of those sessions were reported in two books: "Gods, Demons, and Space Chariots" and "Gods and Devils from Outer Space" by Eric Norman.

One odd fact that was brought out was that the aliens wore uniforms with an emblem of a winged serpent on the left breast, similar to the winged serpents that have appeared in mythology around the world.

Abduction of José Antonio da Silva

Full Report/Article
The following abduction occurred at Bebedouro, Minas Gerais, Brazil, in the afternoon of May 4, 1969. 24-year-old José Antonio da Silva, an enlisted soldier, was fishing on a lagoon when suddenly he heard voices, became aware of figures moving behind him, and felt a burst of light strike his leg. He dropped his fishing rod and fell to his knees.

Date May 4, 1969
Location Bebedouro, Minas Gerais, Brazil

Two beings, about four feet tall, wearing aluminum like suits and what appeared to be helmets, seized him and dragged him to an object sitting on a dirt road. The object was shaped like an upright cylinder and had black platforms at each end. The soldier was taken inside, where the beings put one of their 'helmets' on him...

Da Silva felt the craft rise. The beings talked animatedly among themselves in a language he did not recognize. After a long period of travel, he felt a jarring that suggested their craft had landed. The soldier was then blindfolded and led to a large room, where they removed the wrap from his eyes.

A being stood in front of him who was extremely hairy and slightly taller than the rest. His waist-long hair was reddish and wavy. ... When the others took off their helmets, they were of similar appearance.

Da Silva watched as the beings, at one point more than a dozen, examined his fishing equipment and took one of every item he had in duplicate. Later the witness noticed on a low shelf the bodies of four human men, one black, and became terribly frightened. Later still, the beings gave him a dark green liquid to drink out of a cubical stone glass.

The dwarf leader then began a strange conservation with the soldier, mostly about weapons, which was conducted entirely with gestures and drawings. Da Silva also understood that they wanted him to help in their relations with humans. When the soldier refused, the dwarf snatched the crucifix from the rosary Da Silva always carried with him. As the soldier began praying, a Cristlike figure appeared to him, making revelations.

Shortly afterwards, Da Silva was blindfolded again and taken back to earth. As the craft landed, he felt he was being dragged and lost consciousness. He woke up alone near the town of Vitoria, about 200 miles from where he had been fishing. He was dehydrated and hungry, but drank from a stream and was able to catch some fish as he still had his rod with him. Only his identity card, which the aliens had examined, had disappeared. He had a swollen knee where the ray had struck him and three open wounds on his neck where the helmet had rubbed against his skin. He had been away four and a half days.

Abduction at Medicine Bow National Park

Full Report/Article

This very interesting case took place in Medicine Bow National Park, Wisconsin. On October 25, 1974, one Carl Higdon was elk hunting in the northern section of the park. As he shot his rifle at an elk nearby, a most bizarre thing happened. The bullet travelled in slow motion, as if he had entered another dimension; it fell some 50 feet away, dropping into the snow covered landscape. He felt a strange sensation over his body.

Date October 25, 1974
Location Medicine Bow National Park, Wisconsin, United States

To his utter shock and amazement, he saw a humanoid entity standing nearby. The humanoid was quite tall, at over six feet in height. He was clad in a black jump suit with a wide belt. The belt was decorated with a six-pointed star and emblem of yellow. With straight hair standing out from his head, he had no eyebrows or chin. He stood bow-legged with long arms ending with rod like appendages instead of hands. The humanoid spoke to Higdon, asking him if he was hungry. The entity threw some pills to him, telling him if he took one, he would not have to eat for 4 days. Higdon normally did not take any type of pills, yet he swallowed one of the offerings immediately. It was surmised that the entity was smart enough to realize that Higdon may have been hungry, or else he would not have been hunting elk.

Soon, the alien pointed toward Higdon, and the next thing he knew, he was enclosed within a transparent apparatus, with a helmet on. Also present were two more humanoids, and the five elk he was previously stalking. The elk were in a frozen state. He was told that the aliens were travelling to their home planet, located some 163,000 light years away. In a flash, they had arrived at the distant location.

Higdon described the surrounding landscape occupied with buildings like the Seattle space needle, all lit up by a sun of intense power. This brightness of the atmosphere caused Higdon's eyes to water, along with the aliens'. Higdon's next remembrance was being back in Medicine Bow Park. He says that approximately 2 1/2 hours had elapsed since his encounter with the humanoid had begun.

He was in a hysterical state, cold, and disoriented. For a time, he could not locate his truck, finally finding it some three miles from where he had left it. It had been stuck in a mud hole, and Higdon was unable to free it from the bog by himself. Using his CB radio, he summoned help from the local sheriff, who arrived at midnight. Additional help arrived to free the stuck truck.

Hidgon was found in a state of panic and nervous exhaustion. He was shouting, "They took my elk!" He was taken for medical care to a local hospital. His blood work showed he had a highly elevated level of vitamins, probably from the pill he had taken. The most fascinating aspect of his tests was that tuberculosis scars on his lungs were now gone!

Further investigation into the details surrounding the bizarre encounter revealed that Higdon's wife, along with two other people had seen a red-green-white flashing light moving in the area of the sighting. The case was investigated by Dr. Leo Sprinkle, Professor of Psychology, University of Wyoming. Also included were Rick Kenyon, and Robert Nantkes, MUFON field investigators, and Frank Bourke, National Star Investigator.

Man Taken into Craft, Encounter with Three Beings

Full Report/Article

This case is actually in the embryonic state — it has just come to our attention and has not been fully investigated to date. APRO is grateful to Field Investigator Jorge R. Martinez of Bahia Blanca, Argentina for the basic information bearing on this case and to Peter Romaniuk of the Institute Biophysica and Jane Thomas for the translation.

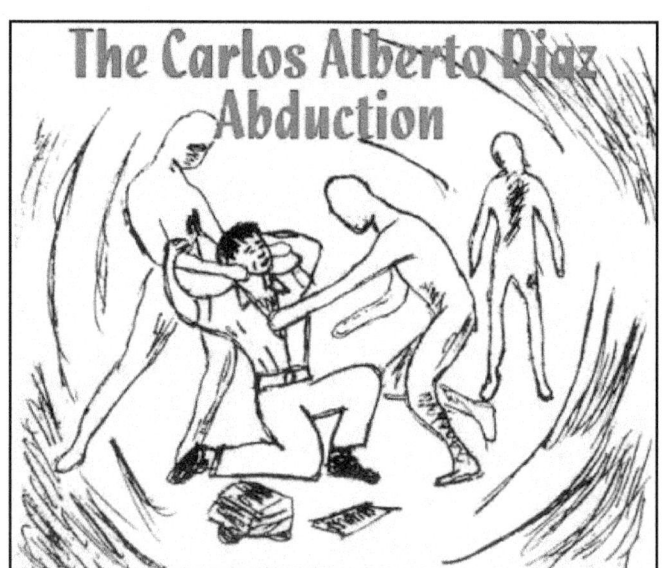

Date January 4, 1975
Location Bahia Blanca, Argentina

Carlos Alberto Diaz is a 28-year-old married man, father of one child and born in Ingeniero White, a district of Bahia Blanca, Province of Buenos Aries, Republic of Argentina. His work record indicates that since becoming an adult he was a clerk in a central store and for 6 years was employed in the mechanical traction section of Ingeniero White. During the past year he helped with the preparation of a football training school for the Huracan Club of Bahia Blanca and in his spare time augmented his income by working as a waiter at private parties.

On the morning of January 4, 1975 he was finishing his shift as a waiter in the Holy Protective Society of the Naposta District in Bahia Blanca. Outside the door he purchased a "La Nueva Provincia" (The Province News) newspaper, then caught the bus to go home. He got off the bus several blocks from his home and started walking. His route was through a large and desolate railroad yard. The sky was overcast so when a brilliant flash of light momentarily blinded him, he assumed it was merely lightning from the approaching storm. .Thunder did not follow, however, and he later described the light as not straight but "broken". After he regained his sight he was frightened and decided to run the rest of the way to his home which was now in sight but couldn't move — he seemed to have become paralyzed.

At that point Diaz heard a humming sound which he compared to the sound of rushing air or wind and his strange experience continued. Although he tried to resist, Dias was pulled off the ground and when about 3 meters (about 8 feet) off the ground he became unconscious. His vision faded before he fainted.

When Diaz regained consciousness he was inside a smooth, bright sphere which appeared to be semi-transparent plastic. There was no furniture or devices and the illumination seemed to come from the walls. Diaz said he was completely lucid and conscious, half kneeling and half lying on his side against several openings of about 3 centimeters in diameter (1-1/4 inches) in the bottom of the sphere through which issued air. He said he felt ill if he turned away from the openings and felt they served to keep him conscious. He estimated the "sphere" was 2-1/2 to 3 meters (about 7X8 feet) in diameter.

Suddenly, Diaz reports, three creatures resembling humans

came sliding into the sphere. They appeared to be 1.75-1.80 meters in height (approximately 5 feet, 10 inches), their heads half the size of a human head and completely devoid of features - no ears, nose, mouth or eyes. The head was mossy green in colour and the body which was rather thin, was covered with something Diaz defined as rubber - light cream coloured and very soft and the creatures were completely hairless.

The arms were almost straight and very flexible and ended in "stumps" rather than hands and fingers.

When the creatures came into the sphere, they immediately began pulling tufts of hair from Diaz's head. He didn't know how they did it, at first, not having hands or fingers, but each time they would reach out their arms would pull back and they would have some of his hair. This seemed to give them great pleasure for they would then jump up and down and wave their arms.

Diaz tried to resist the creatures but to no avail. During his struggles Diaz felt the softness of their bodies and ultimately noted they had "suckers" on their arms and assumed that was the method by which they removed the hair. One of them held him, another pulled his hair and the third apparently only observed. Diaz noted the fact that he felt no pain as they pulled at his hair, both on his head and chest. The creatures moved slowly but were very strong and seemingly tireless, he said.

After this ordeal was over, Diaz's sight began to wane gradually and he then fainted. He remembers nothing else of the experience.

Several hours went by and Diaz woke up and found himself lying on the grass and had to close his eyes as the sun was high and shining into them. He was fully recovered and conscious and near a large, busy highway. Diaz looked at his watch which had stopped at 3:50, the time he last noted before his experience began. Beside him was his bag containing his work clothes and the newspaper he had bought hours before. Diaz felt ill and this illness stayed with him throughout the day.

A man appeared driving a car on the adjacent highway which was 30 meters (about 100 feet) from Diaz's location. The man thought Diaz had been struck by a car and stopped. Upon hearing Diaz' explanation of what had happened to him, he offered to take him to the nearest hospital (Railway Hospital), where they arrived

25 minutes later at 8:30 A.M. It was when he learned the time that Diaz became convinced that he had been abroad an aircraft of unknown origin and in the company of extraterrestrials.

For the next four days Diaz was confined to the Ferroviaro Hospital in Buenos Aires, Argentina where he was questioned and examined again and again by 46 different doctors. The hospital's Director informed the Federal Police who also questioned Diaz.

Diaz's wife and other relatives were notified by telephone at 9:20 A.M. They had been extremely worried because Diaz seldom arrived at home later than 4:00 or 4:30 A.M. They went to Buenos Aires that day, arriving at about midnight. It is 785 kilometers (423 miles) from Bahia Blanca to Buenos Aires.

The examination of Diaz yielded no evidence of physiological or psychological alteration in Diaz, except the illness described as dizziness, upset stomach, the lack of appetite and the missing hair. During the 5 th of January Diaz had only one cup of milk which had to be fed to him forcibly.

We are immediately struck by three similarities in the Higdon and Diaz cases, namely: in both instances, the "creatures" had no hands or fingers and in both cases the witnesses suffered a loss of appetite after the experience and lastly, the entities in both cases "glided" rather than walking.

As we have pointed out in this Bulletin in the past, we must consider the possibility of deliberate confusion in these cases of absolutely bizaare (to us) creatures and experiences. It seems likely in Higdon's case that he was under the influence (both he and his gun) of something when he went over the crest of that hill and saw the elk. In Diaz's case, he was rendered unconscious before his experience with the humanoids began. Was he also under some kind of influence? Obviously something unusual happened to him — the absence of hair in various spots on his head and chest attest to that. If we speculate that he pulled his own hair out, for whatever reason, we must then consider the fact that, outside of one interview with a magazine, he permitted no interviews with newspapers, radio or TV and was questioned by only one civilian UFO investigator — Mr. Romaniuk. He obviously did not thirst for publicity or motoriety. Then we have the problem of how he got from Bahia Blanca to Buenos Aires in a matter of 4 hours and 10 minutes — a distance of 423 miles. In the United States, travelling on the best of the roads and breaking speed limits, the best that could be done would be something over 5 hours. Diaz does not own a car. We can rule out cars and of course, buses. That leaves only air travel. Did Carlos Diaz get a flight from Bahia Blanca to Buenos Aires? This will have to be checked. We must also check to make certain that Diaz was on the job and left at 3:30 - as he claims. We must also verify that he was, in fact, on the city bus and did get off at a point a few blocks from his home.

There have been alleged cases of transportation of humans by UFOs in the past, but Carlos Diaz's alleged experience appears to be one of the most credible of them all.

Travis Walton Abduction Case

Full Report/Article

On November 5, 1975, six young woodcutters, along with their employer, were working in the Apache-Sitgreaves National Forest, engaged in a tree-thinning contract for the U. S. Forest Service. The forest is located in east central Arizona, and the work area is fifteen miles from Heber.

The story begins at approximately 6:10 P.M., when the men were heading home in a seven-man crew-cab truck. Travelling along a bulldozed trail, one of the men sighted a gold-coloured glow through the thickets. As they rounded a right-hand turn, they saw the source of the glow - a structural object hovering approximately fifteen feet above a clearing and a scant ninety feet or so from the viewers.

Date November 5, 1975
Location Sitgreave-Apache National Forest , Arizona, United States

Travis Walton, 22, was sitting on the right-hand passenger side of the front seat. When he saw the object, he called to Mike Rogers, the driver and boss of the crew, to stop. Hardly waiting for the truck to come to a complete halt, Walton jumped out and, at a fast walk, approached a woodpile (stacked by the thinners) to get a closer look. As his fellow employees called for him to be careful and come back, he stood and looked at the object, which was at a 60-degree elevation from his position. It had the shape of two "pie pans" or shallow bowls placed rim to rim. A "beeping" sound was heard by all.

Walton stepped back a couple of paces, intending to vacate the vicinity of the craft when his friends were startled to see a blue-green beam shoot out from the bottom of the craft, striking Walton in the upper area of his body, lifting him from the ground with his arms out stretched, and flinging him back to the ground.

Thinking he and the others were in danger, Rogers restarted the truck and left the area. A quarter of a mile away, he stopped and the six men looked back. They saw a light rise from the ground and streak into the north east, originating in the area where they had left Travis. Thinking it was the object; Rogers turned the truck around and drove back to the clearing.

For fifteen minutes the men searched for Walton, covering the near area and calling, but to no avail. Rogers then decided to drive to Heber, the nearest town, and report Walton's disappearance to the sheriff. On the way, they debated what they should tell, doubting that the truth would be believed, but, unable to come up with an acceptable explanation, they told what they had experienced.

On November 10, the six men were given polygraph tests which established that they had not harmed Walton (it had been implied that they had done away with Travis and hidden his remains, despite the fact that Rogers was his best friend of many years standing) and that they had, actually, seen a UFO.

On the night of November 10, at approximately midnight, a call came in to the Grant Neff residence (Mrs. Neff was Travis' sister and at the time the only Walton in Snowflake, Arizona, with a telephone). It was Travis, sounding confused and disoriented, saying he was at a phone booth in Heber and in terrible pain. Neff went to Mrs. Kellett's (Travis' mother) home, picked up Travis' brother Duane, who had come up from Phoenix when notified of his brother's disappearance, and drove at breakneck speed to Heber, where they found Travis slumped in a phone booth. He had a five-day growth of beard and appeared thin but was otherwise apparently all right.

Within hours, Duane drove Travis to his home in Phoenix, intent on keeping him away from the horde of reporters, which had plagued the Walton family during Travis' disappearance, and to obtain medical treatment.

For a short time, Duane Walton was frustrated by the representative of a local UFO group, who sent him to a pseudomedical hypnotist, but he was eventually contacted by the Aerial Phenomena Research Organization (APRO), which called in a team of medical experts.

Ultimately, Walton was given the Minnesota Multi Phase Personality Inventory (MMPI), Rorschach (commonly called Inkblot) Polygraph and Psychological Stress Evaluator tests, all of which established that he had told the truth as he knew it. All of these tests were conducted and interpreted by experts.

Unfortunately, Walton only recalls an hour or two of his five-day absence. He claims to have awoke on a table in a room which he first assumed was a hospital. The ceiling seemed low, there was an oval-shaped metallic-coloured apparatus on his chest (his denim jacket and shirt were pulled up), and he was in considerable pain. The "air" in the room seemed oppressive, i.e., warm and damp. It took a few minutes to get his wits about him, and when he became fully aware of his surroundings, he realized he was in no ordinary hospital. Around the "table" on which he reclined were three strange creatures-strange, because they were less than five feet tall, very pale, with large, domed heads, large eyes, small nose, mouth, and ears, and their bodies, encased in tannish orange, seamless jumpsuits, and were very thin.

Upon seeing them, Walton struggled to his feet, and when they approached him with their fingernail-less hands outstretched, he grabbed a rodlike object from an adjacent table and prepared to defend himself. After flailing about with the instrument for a moment or two, Walton was surprised to see the trio file out of the door and turn to the right.

After the creatures left, Walton also exited the room, turning left. Following a curved corridor, looking for a way out, he found a circular room with a chair (which was too small for him but nevertheless he sat in it) with a "screen" on each arm. He touched a lever and the "stars" on the "ceiling" above seemed to move, so he moved the lever back to its original position and decided against further experimentation.

Shortly, a "man," approximately six feet tall, with brown hair and strange golden-brown eyes, appeared at the door which Travis had entered. He beckoned to Travis, and Travis went to him, babbling question after question, none of which were answered. The "man" said nothing, took Travis by the arm, led him out into the corridor or hall, to the right, then stopped, whereupon a section of the wall opened. He had not touched anything. They walked into a small room, the door behind them closed, and seconds later a door opened in front of them. They then went down an incline (apparently out of the enclosure Walton had been in) where Walton found himself in a large enclosure resembling a quarter of a cylinder. There were three or four oval-shaped metallic objects parked there (the same apparent metallic substance as everything else he had seen). He was led by the "man" (who was clad in a blue "jumpsuit" with a clear "helmet") through the enclosure, to another door into a room where there were three other human-appearing individuals-two men and a woman. They resembled the first, except that, although they wore the same clothing, they were without helmets.

They gestured to him to get upon a table. He resisted, but they eventually succeeded in their efforts and Travis reclined; an apparatus resembling an oxygen mask with a black ball attached was placed over his face and he lost consciousness.

Travis awoke about midnight about a quarter mile west of Heber, Arizona. He was lying on his stomach and raised up to watch the curved, metallic hull of an aircraft taking off straight up, reflecting the yellow stripe of the dividing line of the highway below.

What did Travis Walton see? What did he experience? Tests indicate that he has related his experience truthfully. His book The Walton Experience (1978) will tend to illuminate the reader and enable him to make his own judgment.

Police Constable Alan Godfrey's Abduction in West Yorkshire, England

Full Report/Article

In November and December 1980, the eastern side of Britain was experiencing a major UFO sighting wave. There were chases of UFOs by police cars near the coast, a UFO that overflew an oil rig in the North Sea, and the wave culminated in the famous events on the East Anglian coast at Rendlesham Forest. Just a month before these landings beside those NATO air bases, one of the most impressive alien abduction cases took place in the small Penninemill town of Todmorden, West Yorkshire, right in the centre of Britain's most active window area known locally as "UFO Alley".

Alan Godfrey, with a drawing of the craft. (credit: Evans and Stacy)

Date November 28, 1980
Location Todmorden, West Yorkshire, United Kingdom

Police Constable Alan Godfrey was on patrol on the night of November 28, 1980. Just before dawn he drove along Burnley Road on the edge of Todmorden looking for some cows that had been reported missing. They were only found after sun-up, mysteriously relocated in a rain-soaked field without hoofmarks to indicate their passage.

Giving up his nocturnal hunt, Godfrey was about to go back to base to sign off duty when he saw a large mass a few hundred yards ahead. At first, he thought it was a bus coming towards him that took workers to their jobs in town and that he knew passed about 5:00 A.M. But as he approached, he realized that it was something very strange. It was a fuzzy oval that rotated at such speed and hovered so low over the otherwise deserted highway that it was causing the bushes by the side to shake. The police officer stopped, propped onto his windscreen a pad that was in the patrol car to make sketches of any road accidents, and drew the UFO. Then there was a burst of light, and the next thing he knew he was driving his car again, further along Burnley Road, with no sign of the UFO.

Godfrey turned around and examined the spot where the UFO had hovered. The road was very wet as it had rained heavily earlier in the night. But just at this one location was a circular patch where the roadway had been dried in a swirled pattern. Only when back at the police station did he realise that it was a little later than he had expected - although any missing time was probably no greater than 15 minutes from estimates later taken on site.

Concerned as to possible ridicule, Godfrey at first chose not to make an official report, but changed his mind later that day when he discovered he was not alone. After breakfast that morning, a driver who had been on Burnley Road three miles further out at Cliviger reported seeing a brilliant white object and contacted Todmorden police. The time matched that of Alan Godfrey's. Furthermore, a police patrol from an adjacent force (Halifax) had been engaged in a stakeout for stolen motorcycles on the moors of the Calder Valley and had witnessed a brilliant blue-white glow descending into the valley towards Todmorden shortly before Godfrey experienced his close encounter. Their story, when it reached Todmorden police station, formed a second match.

Encouraged by this news Godfrey filed an official report, but was surprised when police chose to release the story to the local newspaper the following week. From here, ufologists discovered the case and a lengthy investigation was mounted by a Manchester-based UFO group.

Although Alan Godfrey had no further conscious recall of the missing time, he did have increasingly confused memory of the sequence of events surrounding the sighting (with an unexplained image of seeing himself outside the car during the sighting). There was also puzzling physical evidence. His police-issue boots were split on the sole, as if he had been dragged along the floor and they had caught on something. He also reported a previous history of seeing other strange things and having experienced at least one earlier time lapse as a youth—factors that ufologists have come to recognise as common with abduction cases.

When sure that all conscious testimony had been recorded, Godfrey agreed to be hypnotically regressed by a Manchester psychiatrist eight months after the incident. He eventually had several other sessions with different therapists, and his recall in later sessions was video-taped. The doctor refused permission to the UFO group for the first session to be recorded.

The hypnotic testimony is very odd, and Godfrey was never to be sure what really happened. Under regression he told of the bright light stopping the car engine, causing his radio and police handset both to be filled with static and then to be swamped by blinding light as he lost consciousness. His next recall was of being inside a strange room, more like a house than a spaceship, complete with a most unexpected large black dog. He was studied by a heavily bearded man who telepathically conveyed that his name was "Yosef" and whose clothing was very Biblical in nature. Assisting Yosef were several small robot-like creatures "the size of a five-year-old lad" and with "a head shaped like a lamp". They are reminiscent of the "Grays" of UFO lore; although with major differences.

Godfrey was supposedly asked questions, told that he "knew" Josef, and was promised a later encounter. But apparently he was not subjected to the more familiar indignities of abduction stories (especially from the US), such as bodily fluid samples and rectal probes. Although there were periods of missing memory, the hypnotic recall that did emerge was a curious hybrid of mythic images, UFO case elements and dream like sequences.

When asked his opinion as to the reality status of this hypnotic testimony, Alan Godfrey was refreshingly honest. He told me he was certain that the UFO encounter was real, but he could not determine whether the story offered by hypnosis was a dream, a fantasy, reality, or a mixture of all three.

Unhappily, Alan Godfrey suffered terribly after this encounter. When I first wrote up the investigation (just before the regression hypnosis began) for Flying Saucer Review magazine in 1981, I deliberately changed his identity to help protect him; although this was probably futile because the story had already been featured in the local press under Godfrey's real name.

However, despite my refusal to assist them, a tabloid reporter traced the witness and devoted a front-page banner headline article to the story — read by millions over the Sunday lunch—which led to the officer being called to explain himself before his superiors. He was forced to undergo medical investigation to determine his "status", but was pronounced psychologically fit and healthy. Yet after some years feeling that he would never be allowed to forget his sighting, he took advice to honourably resign over an unrelated physical injury incurred during an incident in which he bravely intervened to avert a crime.

Todmorden, both before 1980 and in the years since, has been a hotbed of alien contact activity with several other major encounters having been investigated, including another abduction of a truck driver from Burnley Road only a little further out of Todmorden and on the same highway.

The Salter Encounter

Full Report/Article

In most cases, a UFO abduction is a harrowing, humiliating experience...one that the participant would love to forget. In some cases, however, the abduction process becomes a rewarding one. Such was the case of John Salter Jr. and his son John III. John Jr. a faculty member of the University of North Dakota, was scheduled for a speaking tour of the Southern states. It was in March 1988 when he, accompanied by his son, drove his pickup truck down Route 61 heading for his first engagement. For some unknown reason, John drove his truck off of his scheduled route, and one hour later, the two found themselves travelling in the opposite direction. They decided to take a rest for the night, and continue their trip the next morning.

Date March, 1988
Location North Dakota, United States

The two men were at a loss to understand what had happened the evening before, though they discussed it at length as they continued down their original mapped-out drive. Suddenly the two were shocked to see a shining UFO with a silvery "energy field." The object had just "appeared" over the road they were on. John Jr. and his son both had a "familiar" feeling about what they were seeing, and they began to have flashbacks, which refreshed their minds of the events of the previous day.

They looked at each other, both now aware that the day before they had been stopped dead in their tracks by the object they were now enthralled with. Both men had stepped out of the vehicle as a group of aliens came toward their pickup truck. At first John Jr. thought he was seeing a group of children, until he saw a taller being, which seemed half-human, half-alien. The group of strange beings led the two men away in the direction of the object. The two men, though frightened in one way, felt that the alien beings would not hurt them. John Jr. would later relate that he felt a sense of being protected by the strange entities. He had taken a stumble while they were making their way to the ship, but a type of "energy" kept him from falling and being hurt.

John Jr. and his son were both led into a room with curved walls, where they were placed in chairs which resembled the fold-back type used by dentists. Both men would later recall a feeling of being "immobilized" while they laid back in the chairs, and were examined. John Jr.'s examination began with an implant being inserted into his nostril, remarkably though, without pain. Next an instrument of some kind was injected into the side of his neck, and another one at the top of his chest. He felt the three areas chosen by the beings had a medical significance: the placement related to three glands; the pituitary, the thyroid, and the thymus. John had enough medical knowledge to know the three glands regulated human growth, metabolism, and immunity.

After the completion of the tests, John Jr. felt a strange sense of "bonding" with the strange, alien beings. He also sensed a message which stated they would meet again. These strange circumstances would take even a more bizarre turn after John and his son had returned home. John Jr. noticed a gradual improvement in his overall health. His fingernails and hair grew faster and thicker, and a scar on his forehead began to fade, and eventually almost disappeared. Another amazing fact John Jr. related was that though he was a smoker who struggled with the desire to quit, he now was able to quit without even thinking about it. To both of the Salter men, the abduction seemed to have a happy ending. John Jr. was known as a respectable, professional man, and those who knew him were hard pressed to discount his story, as remarkable as it may seem. The case of the Salters was dramatized on the 1988 CBS movie, "Visitors From The Unknown."

Kelly Cahill Abduction

Full Report/Article

In August 1993, 27-year-old Kelly Cahill, her husband and three children were driving home after a visit to a friend's house. Their routine journey would soon become a harrowing trip into an unknown world of strange beings that occupied space but were void of colour as we know it. The Dandenong foothills, near Belgrave, Victoria, Australia would have its location forever linked to one of the most unusual sightings of a strange creature in Ufology archives. Records from the town of Leicester, England in the year of 1928 give an account of another being without colour. The Cahill family would witness either more of the same, or very similar beings in the wee morning hours of August 8.

Date August 8, 1993
Location Dandenong foothills, Australia

After midnight the Cahills were on their journey home when they first noticed the lights of a rounded craft with windows around it. It silently hovered above the road. Different coloured lights were clearly visible on the bottom of the object. The UFO was so close to the ground that Kelly thought she could see people through the window openings. As she began screaming to her husband what she was seeing, the craft zoomed off to their left, disappearing as quickly as it had made itself known.

Continuing their drive home with a renewed interest in the sky, they suddenly came upon a light ... a light so bright they were practically blinded. Shading her eyes from the intense light with her hands over her eyes, Kelly begged of her husband, "What are you going to do?" Her husband now frightened to death by the glowing presence before them, replied, "I am going to keep on driving." Within what seemed only a second or two, Kelly was now very relaxed, suddenly calmed by the disappearance of the intense, glowing light that had turned night into day for a brief few moments.

The first words out of Kelly's mouth were, "What happened, did I blackout?" Her husband said nothing, as he had no answer to give his wife. He cautiously drove his family home. Upon their safe arrival Kelly could smell a foul odour, like vomit, and she suddenly felt as though something was missing from their drive home. Something was missing...an hour or so of time had vanished from her and her family's life.

That night as Kelly undressed for bed, she noticed a strange triangular mark on her navel, a mark she had never seen before. It must have been created early this very night. But how? And why? And most importantly, by whom? Kelly suffered from general malaise for the next two weeks, and was taken to the hospital on two occasions, one for severe stomach pain, and another for a uterine infection.

Kelly would soon begin to remember details of that fearful night, and without any outside aid such as regressive hypnosis, or counseling. She recalled the object they had seen in a slightly different place than she first remembered. It was hovering in a gully, and the UFO was big. She estimated it at 150 feet in diameter. She could also recall that when the object was first spotted, her husband had stopped the car, and both her and her husband had gotten out of the vehicle, and walked in the direction of the massive craft, without fear. It was if they were being subconsciously drawn to the enigmatic, otherworldly creation.

To their surprise, they noticed another car stopped on the side of the road. As they walked down toward the craft, they saw a creature unlike either of them had ever seen before. It was black, not a black colour but black as if all matter was removed where its presence was. Kelly would later describe it as "not having a soul."

Kelly's words for the alien were "void of colour," yet its shape was clearly discernible. The black alien entity was taller than an average man, about 7 feet tall, according to Kelly, and its eyes were large like a fly's, glowing red. After being mesmerized by the sight of the being, she saw more of them. "Heaps of them" is how Kelly described them as she stared into the open field.

The aliens were out there in the field, beneath the immense flying craft. The beings seemed to congregate in small groups, and one group glided toward Kelly and her husband, covering a hundred yards in a mere few seconds. Another group was approaching the other car which sat motionless near the hovering craft.

Kelly had a sense that the creatures were evil. She clung to her husband, fighting the feeling of blacking out. Her great fear and dread would cause her to scream at the alien-looking entities to leave them alone. She remembered going unconscious, and then ... she was back in their car.

As strange as this encounter seems, it was not without corroboration. The occupants in the other car would come forward and tell almost an exact story, a story of abduction, mind control, and embarrassing procedures. Kelly recalled through dreams the black alien stooping over her helpless, nude body like he was kissing her navel. From all indications of the descriptions of the aliens, they were intruding into our dimension, taking space in our universe, yet without solid form, though shapes, heads, eyes, and arms could be distinguished. Could these strange and eerie beings simply slip from a parallel existence into ours? Or were they from a not too distant future?

The account of Kelly Cahill has been examined and reexamined by many researchers. Many theories have been put forward, but nothing new has been uncovered. Nothing has been proven, or disproved. Kelly Cahill was considered a reliable, honest person by those who knew her at the time of this strange sighting. Her case is considered legitimate by many UFO investigators.

World-Wide Abduction Cases

Alien abduction is a world-wide phenomenon, although different types of alien appear in different parts of the world. But because people are becoming more familiar with the language of abductions their stories tend to coincide.

Russian Abduction

Alien abductions even happened in the former Soviet Union. A good communist named Anatoly was walking along the shores of Lake Pyrogovskoye in May 1978 when he was grabbed by two aliens who wore dark suits made out of Cellophane. They took him for a spin in their spacecraft, but it appears that they really just wanted a chat.

He asked them to help the Soviet Union to fight the evils of the world – that is, capitalism, which Anatoly believed caused world-wide poverty. Although they acknowledged that helping the poor was a noble aim, the aliens found the idea impractical: 'If we helped the poor', they argued, 'then we would have to help the not so poor, then we would end up helping everyone'. They gave him a drink which tasted like lemonade laced with salt. If their civilization was so advanced, he asked, why did they not drink vodka? 'Perhaps if we drank vodka we would not be such an advanced civilisation', the aliens astutely replied.

The aliens then kindly dropped him off by the lake. When he got home and revealed to his wife what had happened, she told him to keep quiet about seeing aliens otherwise he may end up doing hard labour in a gulag. However, Anatoly felt that by not reporting the abduction he had not fulfilled his duty to the state and therefore told the local commissar about it. The commissar believed that Anatoly was fabricating the story in order to avoid a court martial. Nevertheless, the proper procedures had to be followed and Anatoly was examined by a psychologist, given a lie-detector test and put under hypnosis. They could find no evidence that he was making it up – in fact, when he described events more fully his story even became convincing. And as he had tried to recruit the aliens to the communist cause they let him off.

African Abductions

During the spring of 1951 a British engineer working in Paarl, near Cape Town in South Africa, had fixed his troublesome car himself and had then decided to take it for a test drive, even though it was late.

He was in a deserted spot halfway up Drakensteen Mountain when he decided to stop, whereupon a very short man dressed in a brown laboratory coat emerged from the shadows. He had no hair, a smooth face and a domed head. 'We need water', he said, in a strange accent. The only water that the engineer had was in the car's radiator, so he took the stranger to a nearby stream. It was then that he saw a huge flying saucer half hidden in the lee of the mountain. The alien was grateful for the engineer's help and invited him aboard. Inside, he was shown a bed, on which another alien was lying.

The engineer was not subjected to a humiliating examination, nor was he offered sex, but the alien said that to recompense for the man's kindness he would answer any questions that he had. Naturally, being an engineer, he wanted to know how the spaceship worked. In response, the alien explained 'We nullify gravity by means of a fluid magnet'. He also asked the alien where he came from, but the alien rather unhelpfully simply pointed to the sky and said 'Up there'.

Also in South Africa, in 1956 the 56-year-old Jean Lafitte was abducted by aliens with large heads and no hair. They paralysed him, before taking him into a room in which he was put on a table and medically examined. During this procedure they implanted something into his brain which would activate his psychic powers, they explained. They said that they were from the Pleiades star cluster and also told him that there was another species of alien visiting Earth from Alpha Centauri. The aliens were not hostile, they said: they had come to lend humankind a helping hand. Over the next 30 years they abducted Lafitte regularly, and in 1986, in the wake of the Chernobyl disaster, told him that they had mopped up the excess radiation spilled by the unclear-power station.

A Rhodesian named Peter met another helpful alien in 1974, when he was driving overnight with his wife Frances from what was then Salisbury, Rhodesia – now Harare, Zimbabwe – to Durban, in South Africa. All of a sudden, on a deserted stretch of road between Umvuma and Beit Bridge, he saw lights in the sky and had the feeling that the car had been taken over by a strange force. Everything fell silent, the scenery looked unreal and the car seemed to be gliding along without touching the road. Peter then fell into a trance and lost all track of time, while Frances slept through the whole experience (maybe her sleep had been induced). Later, they realized that they had lost some time. Furthermore, the car had not used as much petrol as it should have done.

Peter was something of a veteran of close encounters. At the age of 13 he had been on a delivery run with his father, a truck-driver, when they had seen a UFO at Shabani. When they had dropped off the electrical equipment that they had been carrying it was found that all the circuits in the equipment had been destroyed by a power surge. Peter also reported having had dreams of floating, as well as out-of-body experiences.

Under hypnosis, he recalled that during the 1974 experience an alien had been beamed down into the car. Using telepathy, he had shown Peter a laboratory on an alien spacecraft in which aliens experimented on the humans that they abducted. The aliens, he said, were able to appear in any form that the witness found acceptable, and on this occasion – as on so many others – the alien had appeared as a small, hairless human with no reproductive organs.

The alien revealed that there were thousands of them living among humankind. They never interfered directly in human affairs, he claimed, but instead tried to influence individuals. He said that they had used this influence to change the world in the past and would do so again – perhaps to end war or to introduce 'their way of doing things'. Yet the alien's various explanations about where he came from were not consistent. At one point he said that he and his fellows had not traveled across space, but across time: they had 'come back in time to get to the Earth'. He also said that they came from the 'outer galaxies', as well as from the '12 planets of the Milky Way'.

In the early evening of August 15, 1981, in heavily forested area around Mutare, on the border between Zimbabwe and Mozambique, 20 workmen were retuning to their village when they saw a ball of light drifting across their path, lighting up the entire La Rochelle estate. All of the men ran for it except for Clifford Muchena, the head man, who watched as the ball turned into a glowing disc and travelled rapidly over the estate.

The light that the disc gave off was so bright that Muchena feared that it might set the forest on fire and therefore raised the fire alarm. The glowing disc then seemed to set down and three tail beings approached him; they were silhouetted in the glow and he thought that they might be estate workers, so he called out to them. This was the wrong thing to do, because they were aliens. They promptly turned towards him and zapped him with a brilliant flash that hurt his eyes. Then he was assaulted with mind-jarring force and lay dazed and paralysed for some time. When he recovered his senses the aliens and their glowing craft were gone.

Muchena seems to have experienced some missing time, but his native language did not contain the words to describe some of the key concepts needed to explain an alien abduction. (In fact, this deficiency may also be true of the English language). Furthermore, his tribe knew nothing about space travel and did not even believe that men had walked on the moon.

Asian Abductions

In the late evening of October 3, 1978 Hideichi Amano, a 29-year-old snack-bar-owner from Sayama City, Japan, drove to the top of a nearby mountain, where the reception was good, to contact his brother by Citizens' Band (CB) radio. In the back of the car was his two-year-old daughter, Juri.

At the top of the mountain the car's engine cut out and the radio stopped working; next the interior began to glow. Amano stuck his head out of the window, but could see nothing; then he looked over his shoulder to check that his daughter was alright. To his horror, he saw a strange, orange light playing across her body. Suddenly he had the sensation of metal pressing against his head and looked up to see a short alien with a tiny nose. Amano was paralysed; weird images and a hideous, screaming noise flashed through his brain.

When the glow disappeared the car's electrical systems began to work again, but the dashboard clock had stopped and Amano had no idea how much time had passed. Terrified, he started the car and drove away.

Although his daughter was none the worse for the experience, Amano was left with an excruciating headache. He later recalled that the alien had abducted him and had implanted something into his head, which he understood would vibrate the next time that they came to get him.

An even more disturbing tale comes from India. In a rural area in 1958, an Indian businessman and his companion saw a flying saucer land in broad daylight and four aliens 3 feet (91 cm) tall get out; they seemed to have some difficulty in walking. It was later discovered that two boys who had been playing on the rock on which the alien craft had landed were missing. One was subsequently found dead and an autopsy revealed that several of his organs had been removed, as if by an expert surgeon. The other boy was found in a catatonic trance and was taken to hospital, where he survived for five days. He never regained consciousness and was therefore unable to explain what had happened to him.

Not all alien abductors in Asia are so dangerous, however. In June 1969, for example, the 27-year-old Machpud met a beautiful female alien in Bandjar, West Java. She took him back to her spaceship, where, in a brilliantly lit room, she indicated that she wanted to make love to him; he obliged. Apparently, the sex was so good that he lost consciousness, later to awake in the Gunung Babakar Forest to find his clothes distributed across a tree. Other than acute embarrassment at being found in this way by a passer-by, he suffered no ill effects.

In Malaysia, people are regularly kidnapped by the 'Bunian people' (no known human tribe). According to the Malaysian UFO investigator Ahmad Jamaludin, the Bunian are smaller versions of humans who have a unique property: during an abduction only the abductee can see them.

At 10 A.M. on one morning in June 1982 the 12-year-old Masweti Pilus was going to wash some clothes in the river behind her house when she bumped into a female Bunian around her own size. The sounds of the village faded and Masweti said that it was as if only she and the Bunian woman existed. The Bunian told her that she was going to take her to see a strange land. Masweti had no option but to go with her, yet she was not afraid and the Bunian took her to a beautiful place. She lost all sense of time, which seemed to fly by. Her relatives later discovered her lying unconscious on the ground not far from her home. Two days had passed.

Chinese people do not seem to be abducted, and perhaps with good reason. The truck-driver Wang Jian Min was driving on the road near Lan Xi, in Chekiang province, at 4 A.M. on October 13, 1979 when he almost ran into a parked car. The car-driver told Wang that he had seen a flying saucer on the road ahead and was now too scared to drive on, whereupon the fearless Wang announced that he would lead the way. The road wound to the top of a hill and Wang accordingly drove up the slope slowly. At the top was a dome-shaped craft that gave off an odd, blue glow; two silver-suited aliens about 5 feet (1.5m) tall clad were standing beside it; they were wearing bright light – like miners' safety lamps – on their heads. Wang wondered whether he might be witnessing an optical illusion and switched off his headlights, but the aliens and the craft were still there. Determined to resolve the situation, Wang then rooted around in his truck's cab and pulled out a crowbar, but when he turned to confront the aliens with it they, along with their craft, had gone.

www.ingramcontent.com/pod-product-compliance
Lightning Source LLC
Chambersburg PA
CBHW070331230426
43663CB00011B/2283